NORMAN BEL GEDDES
MAGIC MOTORWAYS

RANDOM HOUSE

CONTENTS

CHAPTER | PAGE

1. Highways and Horizons   1
2. Safety, Comfort, Speed and Economy   15
3. Eliminate the Human Factor in Driving   43
4. Separated Lanes of Traffic   59
5. Every Highway Intersection Is Obsolete   83
6. Full Speed Through Bottlenecks   105
7. Daylight Standards for Night Driving   123
8. From the Atlantic to the Pacific in One Day   141
9. Eliminate Graft and Double Highway Construction   165
10. Motorway Service to Towns and Villages   185
11. Motorway Tributaries to Cities   203
12. Accelerating City Traffic One Hundred Per Cent   221
13. The Need for Increased Distribution   247
14. Thinking for Our Grandchildren   263
15. Effects of a National Motorway System   285

ACKNOWLEDGMENTS

This book could hardly have been written without the invaluable help of Roger Nowland and Worthen Paxton, for whose constant encouragement and able advice I am very grateful; of Joan Geddes and William Harlan Hale in an editorial capacity; of Joseph Goldsen for statistical and historical material; of Peter Schladermundt and Russell Fudge, in assembling the illustrations.

It would be quite impossible adequately to thank all the other individuals and organizations who, in one way or another, have assisted me in the preparation of this volume. The book is the result of five years' concentrated study by members of my organization and people on the outside who have most generously put themselves at our disposal.

I have made liberal use, not always accredited in the text, of the knowledge and ideas of the following organizations:

American Association of State Highway Officials
American Road Builders Association
Automobile Club of Southern California
Automobile Manufacturers Association
Institute of Traffic Engineers
National Highway Users Conference
National Research Council
National Safety Council
Port of New York Authority
Public Roads Administration
Regional Plan Association of New York
State Highway Departments of numerous states, especially New York, New Jersey, Pennsylvania and California
Yale University Bureau for Street Traffic Research

NBG

HIGHWAYS AND HORIZONS

Five million people saw the Futurama of the General Motors Highways and Horizons Exhibit at the New York World's Fair during the summer of 1939. In long queues that often stretched more than a mile, from 5,000 to 15,000 men, women and children at a time, stood, all day long every day, under the hot sun and in the rain, waiting more than an hour for their turn to get a sixteen-minute glimpse at the motorways of the world of to-morrow. There have been hit shows and sporting events in the past which had waiting lines for a few days, but never before had there been a line as long as this, renewing itself continuously, month after month, as there was every day at the Fair.

The people who conduct polls to find out why other people do things, and the editorial writers, newspaper men and columnists who report daily on the doings of the human race, all had their theory as to why the Futurama was the most popular show of any Fair in history. And most of them agreed that the explanation was really very simple: All of these thousands of people who stood in line ride in motor cars and therefore are harassed by the daily task of

ENTRANCE RAMPS TO GENERAL MOTORS WORLD'S FAIR FUTURAMA EXHIBIT

General Motors

getting from one place to another, by the nuisances of intersectional jams, narrow, congested bottlenecks, dangerous night driving, annoying policemen's whistles, honking horns, blinking traffic lights, confusing highway signs, and irritating traffic regulations; they are appalled by the daily toll of highway accidents and deaths; and they are eager to find a sensible way out of this planless, suicidal mess. The Futurama gave them a dramatic and graphic solution to a problem which they all faced.

Masses of people can never find a solution to a problem until they are shown the way. Each unit of the mass may have a knowledge of the problem, and each may have his own solution, but until mass opinion is crystallized, brought into focus and made articulate, it amounts to nothing but vague grumbling. One of the best ways to make a solution understandable to everybody is to make it visual, to dramatize it. The Futurama did just this: it was a visual dramatization of a solution to the complex tangle of American roadways.

As all those who saw it know, the Futurama is a large-scale model representing almost every type of terrain in America and illustrating how a motorway system may be laid down over the entire country—across mountains, over rivers and lakes, through cities and past towns—never deviating from a direct course and always adhering to the four basic principles of highway design: safety, comfort, speed and economy. The motorways which stretch across the model

[4]

Futurama Photo by Richard Garrison

THROUGH MOUNTAINS

Futurama Photo by Richard Garrison

SPANNING RIVERS

Futurama Photo by Richard Garrison

SKIRTING CITIES

Futurama Photo by Richard Garrison

PAST TOWNS

[5]

are exact replicas, in small scale, of motorways which may be built in America in the near future. They are designed to make automobile collisions impossible and to eliminate completely traffic congestion. Particular features of the motorways may perhaps be improved on, details of future road construction and engineering may differ, but the design of these motorways has been carefully and thoughtfully worked out and is suggestive of probable future developments.

Much of the initial appeal of the Futurama was due to its imaginative quality. But the reason that its popularity never diminished was that its boldness was based on soundness. The plan it presented appealed to the practical engineer as much as to the idle day-dreamer. The motorways which it featured were not only desirable, but practical.

As each spectator rode around the model in his comfortable, upholstered armchair, he listened to a description of it in a voice which came from a small speaker built into the back of the chair. This recorded description synchronized with the movement of the chairs and explained the main features of what was passing before the spectator's eyes. It directed his attention to the great arterial highways which were segregated into different speed lanes and which looked so different from the roads of today. It pointed out the overpasses, high-speed intersections and wide bridges over which tear-drop motor cars whisked by at a hundred miles an hour. It commented in passing on the surrounding scenery, the planned cities, decentralized communities and experimental farms. But it did not describe in detail how any of this was to be accomplished. It did not explain how the highway system worked. It could not dwell at length on any specific points of interest because of the short time available.

There was much more to see, and no time to see it. There was much more to explain, and no time to explain it. Millions of people, by waiting patiently for

[6]

Futurama Photo by Richard Garrison

STREET INTERSECTION—CITY OF TOMORROW—WORLD'S FAIR 1939

their turn in the chairs, demonstrated that the prospects of America's future concern them. They showed that the problems of transportation vitally interest them. But there was no time to satisfy that interest fully. They saw the world of tomorrow lying there invitingly before them—a world that looked like Utopia and that did not seem to have a very close relation to the world they knew. But they weren't let in on the secret of how it had developed; they weren't told how it worked.

This book will take you backstage. It will answer the many questions which the Futurama left unanswered. The Futurama and this book are two different treatments of the same material. The book is a description of the exhibit, just as the exhibit is an illustration of this text. And the book will do two things which the Futurama could not do. First, it will describe the premises, based on American experience, on which such a future transportation system is built; and second, it will suggest the consequences, technical and economic and social, which will result from such a future transportation system. Starting from the facts of congestion, confusion, waste and accidents, we have gone through analysis and blueprints until we have come out on the other side with an over-all plan. We have come out with transcontinental roads built for a maximum of one hundred and a minimum of fifty miles an hour. We have come out with cars that are automatically controlled, which can be driven safely even with the driver's hands off the wheel. We have discovered that people could be driving from San Francisco to New York in twenty-four hours if roads were properly designed. Peering through the haze of the present toward 1960 is a great adventure. It is an adventure so broad in its attack and so far-reaching in its consequences that there is no reason why each reader, layman as well as expert, should not repeat it now for himself and discover where it leads.

Futurama Photo by Richard Garrison   PLANNED MIDWEST METROPOLIS 20 YEARS FROM NOW

In designing the Futurama, we reproduced actual sections of the country—
Wyoming, Pennsylvania, California, Missouri, New York, Idaho, Virginia
—combining them into a continuous terrain. We used actual American cities
—St. Louis, Council Bluffs, Reading, New Bedford, Concord, Rutland,
Omaha, Colorado Springs—projecting them twenty years ahead. And we of
course took already existing highways into account, making use of their most
advanced features and, at the same time, projecting them also twenty years
ahead.

There are many highways which strike us today as excellent—among
others, the Merritt Parkway in Connecticut, the boulevard through the Great
Smokies in the Southeast, the highway over the Santa Cruz Mountains in
California, and New York City's great system of approaches and peripheral

highways. In comparison with what we have had in the past, these are fine roads, representing a tremendous advance over the roads of yesterday. But the roads of tomorrow will represent an equally great advance over those of the present, and it is toward this future development that the Futurama pointed the way.

The Motorway System as visualized in the Futurama and described in this book has been arbitrarily dated ahead to 1960—twenty years from now. But it could be built today. It is not too large a job for a generation which has replaced the plodding horse and buggy with the swift-moving automobile, which has grown wings and spanned the world with them, which has built skyscrapers a thousand feet high. Modern engineering is capable of magnificent accomplishments.

Already the automobile has done great things for people. It has taken man out beyond the small confines of the world in which he used to live. Distant communities have been brought closer together. Throughout all recorded history, man has made repeated efforts to reach out farther and to communicate with other men more easily and quickly, and these efforts have reached the climax of their success in the twentieth century. This increasing freedom of movement makes possible a magnificently full, rich life for the people of our time. A free-flowing movement of people and goods across our nation is a requirement of modern living and prosperity.

People who have achieved a partial success are often inclined to sit back self-satisfied and blind themselves to the fact that the success is only partial. Because we today move more freely than our ancestors, we have a tendency to overlook the fact that we should be able to move ten times more freely. We are satisfied with the mere possession of

MEN, MACHINES OR SHEEP?   Ewing Galloway

the automobile, and fail to make use of its full potentialities. Many of us do not realize that our cars can reliably do up to eighty-five miles an hour, but that the average speed of motor traffic in the United States is twenty miles an hour; that although our cars have been designed for efficiency and economy, the loss due to traffic congestion in New York City alone is a million dollars a day; that although our cars have been designed for safety, there is a death toll on American roads today of almost four lives every hour, ninety every single day, 2,700 a month, and 32,400 a year! Until recently, we have been told that the cure for these paradoxes lies in hit-or-miss, spasmodic road "improvements" and catchy safety slogans. But we are due to open our eyes any day now, and demand a comprehensive, basic solution to a comprehensive, basic problem.

If a word-association psychologist asked you to speak the first word that comes into your head after you hear the word "traffic," you would probably answer, not "flow" or "movement," but "congestion." You would get a mental picture of the crowded approach to the Eads Bridge in St. Louis over the Mississippi, or of cars jammed bumper to bumper at the intersection of State and Madison in Chicago, or perhaps just of a suburban crossroad and the accident that occurred there last Saturday after the Country Club dance. The word "traffic" is usually taken to mean "too many cars." But, actually, traffic is simply the flow of cars along a road, and roads are supposed to be built to accommodate that traffic. When traffic is congested, the answer is not that there are too many cars, but that the roads have not been designed to perform

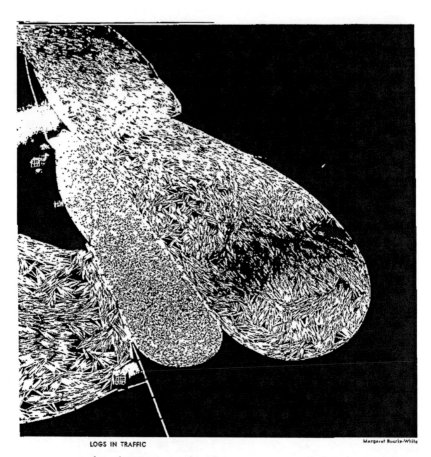

LOGS IN TRAFFIC Margaret Bourke-White

their function properly. Their construction and design are inefficient.

The real trouble with American highways is the simple fact that they are not designed for the traffic they bear. The automobile has advanced in much greater strides than have roads. It has attained a far greater point of perfection. Automobiles are in no way responsible for our traffic problem. The entire responsibility lies in the faulty roads, which are behind the times.

When the horse was discarded, the winding roads over which he joggled were not discarded with him. The automobile inherited them. Some of them have been "improved" from time to time, but their basic features have remained unchanged. The result of pushing motor cars out over these old roads was at first simply a mild havoc and runaway horses, but later, the Traffic Problem. Today we are still rebuilding old roads that were constructed for another vehicle, instead of starting to build special roads for the special needs of the automobile.

This simple fact is the key to the whole present-day traffic problem.

A brief glance at the history of road building in this country will make clear how vitally this anachronism has affected the development of American automotive transportation.

SAFETY, COMFORT, SPEED AND ECONOMY

2

IN LAYING out roads, certain basic principles are always followed. From the beginning of time, whenever people have tried to get from one place to another, they have kept these same basic aims in mind. The first is their desire for self-preservation; the second is their desire for a pleasant trip; the third is their desire to reach their goal quickly; and the fourth is their desire to spend as little money and effort on the way as possible.

Now, for self-preservation, read *safety*; for a convenient and pleasant trip, read *comfort*; for a quick arrival, read *speed*; and for a saving of expense and effort, read *economy*; and you have the four main principles which guide—or should guide—the modern road builder.

Although these aims or principles are very specific, their application with reference to road development varies with enormous latitude. A bird flying from one point to another, never swerving to right or left, is following the principles of safety, comfort, speed and economy as he sees them. On the other hand, a man in a forest, moving slowly, twisting first this way then that way, avoiding dangerous ledges and carefully going out of his way to pass around

SAFE (IN THE ARMS OF JESUS)

COMFORT (LOVES COMPANY)

SPEED (AND A YARD WIDE)

ECONOMY (IF YOU'VE NOTHING TO DO)

obstacles, is applying the same principles as he sees them. Several factors enter into the situation, requiring, if not modification of the principles, at least different methods of carrying them out. The rate at which one is capable of moving, the characteristics of the terrain over which one must travel, and the purpose of the journey are some of these modifying factors.

A mountain goat, marvelously sure-footed, nonchalantly travels along the narrow edge of precipitous cliffs which a man must avoid. A cow, fat and lazy, meanders zigzag across a field which another animal would traverse in half the time. A sailboat tacks first north, then south, to reach a destination toward which a steamship can aim directly. Different types of vehicles require different types of routes, in order to achieve the same ends. What is comfortable in a slow vehicle may well be uncomfortable at a fast pace; similarly, a speed which is perfectly safe in one vehicle might be disastrous in another.

It follows from this that each type of vehicle should have its own specifically designed path. The cow has its gently winding path, the wagon its wider, straighter road, the train its railroad track, the ship its sea lane, the barge its canal, the airplane its beacon lanes. Sometimes it happens that a route which was originally intended for one purpose can be adapted to another, but generally the changes which are made in the route to facilitate this adaptation end by altering it beyond recognition. It is hard to realize, for example, that many of America's most important automobile roads originated as animal tracks.

When the first white settlers moved in to open up the Middle West, they did not have to build for themselves the roads which carried them out there. They used routes already there: Indian paths and buffalo trails. The American bison, heavy yet fleet of foot, tough and hard-traveling, had torn wide paths east and west, north and south, along the high ground linking the best grazing ranges and water holes. The bison migrated freely, his range extending from the salt licks of Kentucky westward to the Rockies, and from the Cariboo Mountains at the northern end of Alberta, Canada, southward into Texas. The Vincennes Road, which runs slantwise through Chicago today, was originally tramped out by herds of bison bound west from Illinois to the prairies. The three great overland routes from the eastern part of the country to the Central West were also stamped out originally by bison: one, the route through Central New York which was later followed by the Erie Canal; two, the route through Southwestern Pennsylvania from the Potomac to Upper Ohio; and three, the great Cumberland Gap route into Kentucky. All over the world, in fact, man has taken over the routes of animals.

The buffalo and Indian trails in America were useful and comfortable because both animal herd and native tribe usually sought out easy grades and direct courses. They laid their roads along high land, since forests there were thinner and winds tended to sweep the high trails clear of leaves in fall and of snow in winter. All primitive races travel close to the ridges,

TRANSCONTINENTAL ROAD ENGINEERS

relying on the safety of the higher ground. This custom, in fact, is the origin of the term *highway*.

The buffalo is not the only animal whose roads have been followed through the centuries. While the cow is not generally thought of as a traffic expert, in her own way she too has been an outstanding highway engineer. From day to day the path that the cow follows from barn to pasture changes little. Once a path has been broken, the cow follows it year in and year out just because it is

[19]

there. Man of course does the same thing, through force of habit and reliance on precedent. The origin of many roads from farm to farm and from farm to village occurred in somewhat the following way. The cow path was never the shortest distance between two points, but it had the virtue of being a track and a well-worn one. So the farmer himself followed it down to his neighbor's house, and it soon developed into a footpath. Then, by clipping shrubbery and branches along its sides, he was able to ride his horse through it. One day he managed it with a horse and cart; from that it became a wagon road. It served him well. The road gradually extended from door to door toward the town's church, and in a generation it became Main Street. So it is that the cow laid out New York's Wall Street district years ago, and, farther north, Boston's Haymarket Square. As paths grew into wagon roads, this did not mean that they were rebuilt to take care of wheeled traffic. It simply meant that a certain number of wagoners had managed somehow to scrape their way through them.

Three centuries were given in America to this kind of gradual road development. Animal trails slowly became pack-horse routes. By 1750 three roads in Pennsylvania and New York were reported to be worn so broad that two pack-horses could meet and pass without danger to their loads. That was progress! Then the great wagon known as Conestoga made its appearance.

Above: LOCAL ROAD ENGINEERS
Below: WHEN "PLEASURE DRIVING" WAS YOUNG

And when it started bumping over the Alleghenies, the pack-horse trail received a diploma and became a road.

Again, that did not mean that the old route was changed. It had merely been cleared; tree-stumps and rocks still clogged it. To begin with, people then did not know how to construct a road for wheeled traffic. Nor did they have the capital or the organization to do the job. The stagecoach had been in use for fifty years before any real improvement in American roads was made.

GENTLE BRIDGES FOR GENTLE DAYS

Portland Cement Assn.

Instead of building new roads, the old ones were patched and widened here and there in their worst spots, and a few of them were surfaced. But whatever minor changes were effected, the basic technique of laying out the road remained the same: rutty tracks were informally widened by hacking away enough underbrush to give a right of way. This method had inherent difficulties, of course. When larger and heavier vehicles were introduced and sent over routes designed for foot-traveler or animal, the original advantages of the routes were lost. The history of the Boston Post Road illustrates this. This road, which was a major military channel during the Revolutionary War, to-

[21]

day is still the main artery between Boston and New York. Throughout the decades—first for horses, then for wagons, then for stagecoaches, then for fast carriages, and finally for automobiles and buses—it has been widened and rewidened and paved and repaved. But its development has always lagged behind the development of the vehicle, so that it has never been able to serve its purpose efficiently. When Sarah Kemble Knight rode from Boston to New York on it in 1704, it was so narrow that branches brushed her from both sides, and it was so difficult to traverse that it took her eight days to make the trip. Today, when 20,000 cars a day pass over it, they pile up in jams at its narrow bridgeheads, its frequent intersections and its sharp turns.

Early in the nineteenth century, people decided to do something decisive about getting better roads. A speculative fever of private road building hit the nation. In the State of New York alone sixty-seven companies sprang up, to build toll roads or turnpikes. A paved turnpike was laid down from

SHORTEST DISTANCE BETWEEN TWO POINTS—

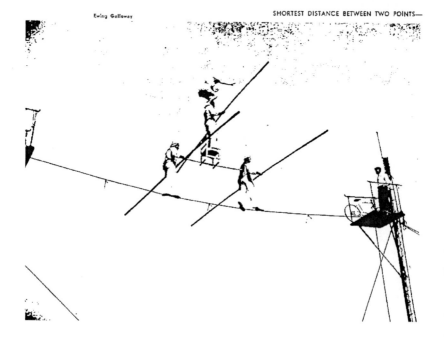

Philadelphia to Lancaster, at a cost of half a million dollars. The Federal Government stepped in and put up money for the Cumberland Road, a national turnpike that tied the Potomac to the heart of the West. Public enthusiasm ran high. Traffic increased.

The Cumberland Turnpike was the culmination of the movement. And it had a curious result. In the push to the West, New York State had been left behind. Accordingly, in order to get a foothold for trade, it set about building the Erie Canal. The Canal was a vast success. It beat the turnpikes at their own game. So the fever for building roads subsided almost as quickly as it had risen, and digging canals became the new national rage. The canal was popular because it was efficient. And it was efficient because it was a right of way built specifically for one means of transit, rather than a makeshift, second-hand adaptation.

The next big step in American transportation came with the introduction

IS NOT ACHIEVED BY CURVES   Portland Cement Assn.

THE IRON HORSE HAD AN IRON ROAD   Acme

of an entirely new vehicle: the locomotive. This proved to be efficient and
popular also, and for the same reason: its builders estimated the needs and
capacities of the new vehicle and designed a right of way for it accordingly.
The first right of way for an American train was laid out on a dirt road
because the train was horse-pulled. But very soon the railroad acquired a
special track adapted to its own functions and its own speed. And the ultimate
result of this intelligent approach to the problem is the safe, efficient and uninterrupted railroad travel of the present day. Not that this result was achieved
immediately; haste in construction often made for waste and mismanagement.
It took about fifty years for the railroads to overcome the first missteps of
inefficiency and planlessness. But the fact remains that their basic technical
approach was sound. The history of American railroads contains many valuable lessons for highway engineers.

Then, just before 1900, another new vehicle appeared. Along the Pumpkin-
ville Pike in Indiana and similar horse roads in Massachusetts, Elwood Haynes
and Charles Duryea were experimenting with the first "horseless carriages."
These "gasoline buggies" did not look very promising at first, and were not
taken very seriously. To say that the country did not recognize the auto for
what it was is to understate the case. The country recognized the auto as a
rattling piece of machinery that could be counted on to break down every

[24]

Southern Pacific Railroad (Sturtevant-Stover)

THE IRON HORSE LEAPS CANYONS

three or four miles. Nobody was going to build a new route for that. A special track had been built for the locomotive, but what had been good enough for the automobile's grandfather was considered good enough for it.

No one seemed to realize that a vehicle was developing which would revolutionize not only all transportation, but life in general. First of all, mechanical transportation was now for the first time being placed at the disposal of the individual to be used whenever he desired, whereas before that time all mechanical transportation had been designed for masses of people only. Secondly, the individual driver was now going to be able to travel two or three times as fast as he had ever traveled before.

THE HORSELESS BUGGY NOSED OUT THE HORSE   Acme

All that three centuries of Americans had done in laying out, widening and brushing up roads suddenly became obsolete. Before this time, travelers had moved so slowly that it never really mattered whether their road was straight or not. No man or animal had ever struck directly across a range of mountains or a river when he could manage to travel around it. In the horse-and-buggy era, no great effort was ever made by road builders to alter or modify the natural character of terrain to reduce the distance between two points, or to smooth out large bumps and recesses. But this new vehicle was capable of high speed. In fact, its entire validity rested on its claim of speed. Curves and bumps that had never bothered the buggy forced the car to slow down. Roundabout routes whose delays had never mattered now harmed the straight-away effectiveness of the car. But this was not understood. The new car was pushed out on the old roads.

Take, as an illustration, the history of one of the world's most heavily traveled stretches of road, the sixteen-mile Detroit-Pontiac Highway. It was in 1817 that its right of way was first laid down, consisting of great logs rolled close together and filled in with clay and sand. By mid-century it had become a plank toll road for horses and buggies. In 1916 it was rebuilt for the automobile—that is to say, it was paved. But its width remained the same as it had been in 1817—a mere sixteen feet. Five years later an observer reported "forty-three automobiles stalled on Sunday afternoon on a stretch of the road badly shouldered by dirt and stones and with a menacing ditch at the side." By 1923 traffic on it had bogged down almost entirely. Then the Governor of Michigan started a piecemeal program of widening it to 200 feet. By 1938, 50,000 people used it every day with what at long last became a high rate of safety—its accident-death rate being less than one-third that of the nation as a whole. Ever since 1817, the State of Michigan had meant well. When it was time for teams and buggies, it built a road for teams and buggies. When it was time for a railroad, it built a railroad bed. But when it was time for motor cars, it patched the road it had already built for another vehicle. It passed laws, hired policemen and set up traffic lights, but it didn't build a proper road for the automobile. What happened here, as well as all over the country under similar circumstances, was that the precept of "economy" overshadowed those of safety, comfort and speed. Three principles were sacrificed for one. But people found that that didn't work.

Almost at the very start of the automobile era, however, there was one interesting exception to this type of highway treatment. In 1906, William K. Vanderbilt II and some cronies who wanted to motor to their Long Island homes at forty miles an hour without scaring horses and infuriating the public, acquired a fifty-mile strip of land 100 feet wide down the island from Flushing to Lake Ronkonkoma. On it they built a two-lane wriggling ribbon of concrete and macadam, on which no carriages were allowed. Because they did not wish to slow down every few hundred yards for a crossroad, they bridged every intersection—which was a brand-new idea. A speed-limitless playground for millionaires was only part of this conception. The important thing about this road was its recognition of the fact that the automobile, in order to function at its best, needs a right of way as free from obstacles as a railroad track.

The career of this Long Island Motor Parkway is interesting. Built at a cost of about $7,000,000 ($140,000 per mile), its original toll charge of one dollar per trip in each direction could not keep it from being a financial failure. Non-millionaire drivers, although enjoying the route as being safe and comfortable and speedy, were aware that instead of being economical it doubled their driving costs over those forty miles. In 1937 the road had to be abandoned. In this way, the lesson that a road must follow all four principles of safety, comfort, speed and economy indivisibly was again pointed out. And at

[28]

the same time it taught another lesson: that unless an idea is thought through in all particulars, it soon grows obsolete. Private enterprise had spent a lot of money on this road, and proved the point that other existing roads were not properly designed for the motor car. When it was first built, the Long Island Motor Parkway was the country's most advanced road. But nevertheless, even its designers did not fully appreciate the possibilities of the automobile. Curves on the Parkway were too sharp, there were too many of them, the road was too rolling, and it was too narrow.

Gendreau

ONE-WAY CAPACITY ON
GRAND CENTRAL PARKWAYS

The gentlemen who built the Parkway might have had more success if they had listened to the wise advice of W. W. Crosby, who urged in 1903 that, before building a road, a traffic census should be taken to determine in advance how much traffic the road would be required to carry. Again in 1914, Engineer S. Whinery urged that roads should be considered in the light of traffic conditions twenty years in the future. This advice also went unheard. The nation's roads still weren't designed for the future at all. They were improved piecemeal to answer immediate needs.

This failure to heed advice led the country to the highway crisis of 1924, when the number of cars on the road reached over seventeen and a half million and motorists came earnestly face to face with the traffic menace. Progressive young engineers wanted to relieve congestion by replanning the whole road system, but public and officials decided differently. They widened the old roads. They set low speed limits on them. They put up thousands of traffic lights. The old ideals of safety, speed, comfort and economy were now being interpreted to read "go slow." It was a far cry from the day when Mr. Vanderbilt had interpreted them to mean "go fast."

[29]

COUNTING TRAFFIC AUTOMATICALLY Acme

While the science of road design was thus being held back, the technique of policing and traffic lights was going forward. In the early nineteen hundreds the major duties required of traffic officers were stopping runaway horses and directing parades. As the automobile began to crowd existing roads and no relief in the sense of newly designed highways was in sight, the policeman grew into a major highway figure. He was stationed in the thick of traffic, and began to require assistants to unsnarl the tangled cars. He resorted to signals, whistles, hand and semaphore devices. In 1924 a series of inventions began dotting the country with various systems of mechanical traffic regulation. Although this represented a contribution to safety, it violated the aims of comfort, economy and speed because it was hit-or-miss, restrictive rather than corrective. What was really needed was a properly designed highway system that would make a maze of traffic lights unnecessary.

Today, with a tremendously multiplied volume of traffic, there is an even greater need for such a highway system. The millions of square miles that make up this country's land, all of its industries, its social development, are all completely dependent on the flow of its traffic—the life-blood of the nation. The medium through which this national life-blood is pumped should be an efficient circulatory system of arteries and veins, instead of three million miles of haphazardly improved routes laid out for the different needs of gold-seekers

in California, of missionaries in the South-
west, fur traders and explorers in the Northwest, covered-wagon pioneers in the Great
Plains, buffaloes in the Middle West and
Indians in New England. Our highway "system" affects the life of each hamlet, city and
farm in the United States, and yet it is still
regarded as a local matter, to be tinkered
with from time to time by state, county and
municipality, as if the blood-stream came to
a stop at the boundary line.

Ewing Galloway

It took years to get the automobile out of
the horseless-carriage stage. The inevitable
conclusion is that highways will have to go
through the same upheaval—sooner or later. And it can be done more safely,
comfortably and economically if it is done soon. But what has been done so
far on the highway, instead of the required upheaval, is a slow process of
adaptation which doesn't work. Mr. R. E. Toms, Chief of the Division of
Design of the Federal Bureau of Public Roads, once said that twenty years
from now motoring will still not be "radically different" from what it is
today, that "the familiar two-lane highway is here to stay," and that "you
won't see any sweeping changes in highway design for years to come." He says
this in spite of the fact that another official in the same Bureau, Mr. H. S. Fairbank, recently admitted that "no single section of our nationwide system of
interstate highways was built for the express use of the automobile." Mr.
Fairbank made this statement in 1938, when there were 30,000,000 cars on
the road, and when experts were estimating that the next twenty years would
double that number. He said this ten years after the installation of the first

James M. Doolittle

FABLE OF THE SNAIL—

AND THE MOTORIST

cloverleaf intersection in the country, after the completion of many "super-highways," "freeways," "skyways" and the like, with all their improvements, and still he was able honestly to say that our highways not only are lagging, but are obsolete.

Automobile travel is less efficient in this respect than any other form of travel. Automobile roads are the only transportation routes which are not systematically planned in accordance with the needs of the vehicles which use them. At sea, for instance, sea lanes are planned for ships. There is nothing haphazard about sea traffic. Guesswork has been reduced to a minimum. The "Great Circle Track," the shortest steaming route between Nantucket Light and Bishop's Rock, England, has been carefully divided into traffic lanes. Ships inform each other by radio of bearing and speed. The channels and aids to navigation have been designed not for the vessels of another day, but for the ships that use them now. In air traffic, too, there is similar planning. Control towers at airports eliminate confusion and congestion. Traffic going in opposite directions is kept apart by regulations allocating it to separate altitudes. The result of this planning is that after a ship has cleared its harbor, or after a plane has climbed to its ceiling, each can proceed to its destination along the best and shortest possible route, without fear of interruption. It can go practically in a straight line. Neither ship nor plane has to use a right of way inherited from some ambling predecessor.

The problems of the railroad are more closely analogous to the problems of the automobile than are those of ship or plane, because both car and train have to travel over land and therefore are subject to inevitable interferences and barriers. But, unlike the highway, the railroad does not give in to this difficulty meekly. In places where financial economy might seem to call for a roundabout route, elaborate engineering is nevertheless usually decided upon to cut through the barrier and

give a direct route, producing greater economy in the long run. The
result is that railroad tracks are a great deal straighter than highways,
and that the train, although inherently a clumsy vehicle, is able to
travel with far greater comfort, safety, economy and speed than the car.

The present-day automobile functions in competition with high-
speed airplanes and locomotives. If there is to be any justification for
its existence, it must match them in efficiency. To do this, it is not
enough to build an efficient automobile—the route is as important to
the vehicle as thread is to a needle. An automobile may be capable of
high speed, but when its road prevents it from using that speed in
safety and comfort—because of steep grades, sharp curves, dangerous
intersections and aimless winding—it is powerless. Therefore, before
re-routing, re-designing or improving an old highway, or before laying
out a new one, the route should always be examined not from the viewpoint of tradition or habit, but with a conscious regard for today's
automobile traffic. In the days of the horse and buggy, economy was
never thought of in terms of time saved or fuel saved. But today that
economy is vital, and the elimination of every unnecessary mile or
hazard counts.

A properly designed highway follows the most direct route that is
available from one point to another; it obeys the old geometric axiom
that a straight line is the shortest distance between two points. That is
a simple, perhaps obvious, statement, and yet if it were really carried
out in practice it would completely transform our highway system. It
is the first guiding principle that should be considered before any high-

MAN IN FLIGHT—BY JOHN COBB   BIRD IN FLIGHT—BY BRANCUSI

way is constructed, before the first plans for it are made.

Chinese road builders purposely place many turns and twists in their roads, because they believe that evil spirits fly along them and that if the roads are crooked enough the evil ones may miss one of the turns, fly off and get lost. Do American road builders also believe in evil spirits? Judging from their handiwork, the answer is yes. Actually, however, the explanation is of course not so simple. The three main obstacles which stand in the way of proper highway design today are: first, the difficulties of acquiring a right of way; second, the pressures and pulls that influence the planning of the route; and third, the terrain over which the route must pass. These three factors have acted as stumbling blocks to all road building organizations, whether Federal, state or municipal. But must they be stumbling blocks for all time to come?

Fortunately, against the piecemeal school of highway construction which generally prevails, there are those students of traffic engineering who can be referred to as "forward-looking men." There have been many who sensed that all was not well with the method of American highway development. Perhaps the credit for the first piece of functional traffic engineering in America should go to Colonel Stephen H. Long, an army engineer, loaned to the Baltimore and Ohio Railroad. This man designed and built a new type of truss bridge which carried the Baltimore-to-Washington roads *over* the railway tracks. Colonel Long named the overpass in honor of Andrew Jackson, then President of the United States. The date was 1830. It was the first attack on the grade crossing.

There were other men who also realized what had to be done. Jay Downer, as Engineer and Executive Secretary of the Bronx Parkway Commission, developed a forty-foot, four-lane highway, eliminated grade crossings, and protected the route from side encroachments. Dr. John A. Harriss did pioneer work on coordinated traffic light systems. Carl Fisher planned the Lincoln

[36]

Highway. Fritz Malcher advanced the "steadyflow" system of traffic. Robert Moses, New York's Commissioner of Parks, has built miles of parkways and the city's Elevated Express Highway.

Various states, too, have seen the alarm signals. New Jersey built the first cloverleaf intersection. Michigan has built highways on the "freeway" principle. Pennsylvania is building a toll highway which will pierce the Alleghenies with nine tunnels, reach heights of 2,500 feet at grades never more than 3 per cent, and maintain a constant highspeed flow with no maximum speed limit, by means of lane segregation, cloverleafs and long sight-distances.

In short, there are a few good roads in America. But not one of them is a patched-up hand-me-down. If we want safety, comfort, speed and economy in travel we must build it into our roads. We must build roads that are literally, not figuratively, motor roads.

There is one famous right of way in America which has recently been built with these ends in view. Its builders had the advantage of starting from scratch, without the heritage of stagecoaches and horses and buggies to establish precedent, and the success of their venture has proved the desirability of starting from scratch. We are speaking of the Hudson River's Holland Tunnel.

Actually, there are two tunnels, one in each direction. Thus traffic moving in opposite directions is completely segregated, visually and physically. There is no cross traffic.

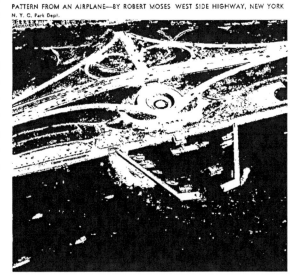

PATTERN FROM AN AIRPLANE—BY ROBERT MOSES WEST SIDE HIGHWAY, NEW YORK
N. Y. C. Park Dept.

Even cars driving in the same direction are required to keep in separate lanes, so that there is no weaving in and out and no sideswiping. Cars are not allowed to stop. All cars must drive at a constant, uniform speed. Each car must keep a standard safe distance behind the car in front of it. The tunnels are always patrolled—not by roaming traffic cops, but by officers so posted that they can see any mishap or failure and report it at once. A wrecking crew is always on call to remove immediately any disabled vehicle. There is no danger of any car striking a pedestrian, for pedestrians move on separated elevated walkways. The margin of guesswork has been reduced by thorough scientific planning. What such planning means comes home to us when we learn that in this one-and-three-quarter-mile tunnel a fatal accident has occurred only once in 47,000,000 motor vehicle miles. If these conditions could be applied to America's entire highway system, our annual automobile death toll, instead of 32,000 lives, would be less than 6,000.

The case of the four gospels of safety, comfort, speed and economy seems to be one of "many are called, yet few are chosen." No one has dared deny these transportation ideals. Many have heeded their soundness. But relatively few have carried them out. Since these words get more lip service on our highways than actual observance, one cannot do better than repeat and redefine them, hoping to drive them home.

SEGREGATED, REGULATED SPEED IN THE HOLLAND TUNNEL   Port of New York Authority

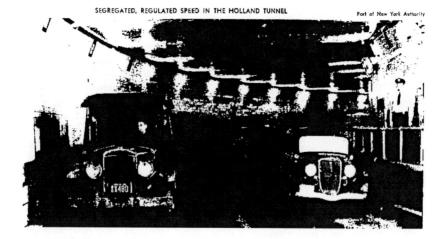

SIMPLE MECHANISM FOR ELIMINATING FLAT TIRES

By safety is meant the safe guiding of the individual along the highway, not necessarily the features which make that safety. By comfort is meant a high degree of ease—though not the ease which is represented by travel in a well-upholstered seat behind a soft-purring, high-powered engine through a jungle of roadhogs, football crowds, bumps, detours and glaring headlights. Comfort must be built into the highway as well as into the automobile. Speed is of course the time it takes to travel, and is achieved not only by building fast-moving automobiles but by laying out highways along the short-est possible distance between two points. Economy must be achieved not only in the financial sense, but in a broader scientific sense: the economy of time and energy as well as of money. And finally, each of these four principles, in order to function fully, has to be combined with the other three. A highway which follows one of these goals at the sacrifice of the other three cannot be an efficient motorway. It may be called a highway—for that term, after all,

CEILING ZERO

Emanuel M.

means nothing more than that the road is laid along high ground. But it is not a motorway—for that word means a right of way explicitly designed for and adapted to the uses of *motor* traffic.

The aim of highway engineers in the twentieth century should be to construct motorways instead of highways. It is an important task, and an inspiring one. It means pioneering, traveling over uncharted territory instead of following in the well-worn paths which tradition has laid down. But just as the horse and buggy have been replaced by the motor car, so must the highway be replaced by the motorway.

ELIMINATE THE HUMAN FACTOR IN DRIVING

GRIM PLEASURE AT THE TURN OF THE CENTURY

Brown Bros.

WHEN a family took a pleasure spin in the car thirty years ago, elaborate preparations were required. Tow ropes, tire-patching outfits, reserve cans of water, oil and gas were provided against the emergency which was likely to happen. A basket luncheon was made ready, to bolster morale when the car broke down in some remote place perhaps fifteen miles from home. Each member of the family was protected from dust. Women didn't drive cars in those days; but they bundled themselves in mummy-like veils for protection. The head of the family cut an even more formidable figure when he appeared in front of the car. Like his wife, he wore a long linen duster, to which he added a cap that would not blow off, goggles of the largest size and special automobile driving gauntlets. Ready to start, the driver approached the car, bent over, put his shoulder firmly against the radiator, mustered up all his strength and spun the crank. Nothing happened. He tried again. If the car backfired, the crank might knock him flat, might break his arm. Any way you looked at it, it was a hazardous matter.

Today, without giving it a thought, the driver steps on the self-starter or

Above: 1905
Below: 1940

presses the starting button on his instrument panel, and the chore is performed for him. The least possible human effort is involved. No year has passed without the introduction of devices to promote safer and more efficient driving. Automatic wipers sweep across windshields made of non-shatterable glass. High-power electric headlights have replaced the gas and kerosene light of earlier days. Automatic tail lights flash warning when the brakes are applied. Four-wheel brakes stop the car. Steel top and body minimize the damage in case of crash. The irreversible steering wheel and shock absorbers help to make driving steady and easy. Tires are now made puncture proof and skid proof. The car which stands in an automobile showroom today is emi-nently safe and easily adapted to human needs. The purchaser of this car considers it very good indeed, and his confidence that each year's car will be better than last year's model is justified by experience.

But how about the driver? Has he too improved in these thirty years of motor-car experience as the car has improved? Not by any means. He is still, day in, day out, on three million miles of road, the same, as bad a driver as the fellow who drove a Chalmers in 1910. His eyesight is no better, he reacts no faster, he doesn't think any better, he gets drunk just as easily, he is just as absent-minded.

Hard-surfaced roads and closed cars have enabled him to lay aside his ponderous dust-protective costume. Today he may never take the wrenches out of his tool kit from one year's end to another. The car that he drives can go three times as fast as the one he had before. Traffic volume has multiplied a hundredfold.

A vast variety of constantly new road situations flash upon him, each of which he must be ready to solve. To keep pace with the machine he manages, he should be able each year to see more clearly, think more quickly and act faster than ever before. His car has been entirely remodeled. His highway is being remodeled. How can the driver be remodeled?

Thirty years ago the worst problem a driver ever encountered was the maximum speed of a runaway horse—and there was practically no congestion problem. Yet even then he had troubles in handling his vehicle. Today the situation is far worse, because he is still the same human being, and yet he has to handle both increased traffic congestion and increased speeds.

No two drivers can be counted upon to behave alike. At the outset that illustrates the seriousness of the problem. Nothing magnifies the difference between individual reactions more than motoring. Even the same man faced with the identical situation at different times will react differently, due to countless factors within himself. Nervousness, irritability and quirks of character so slight that they ordinarily pass unnoticed become positive dangers at motor speeds. Absent-mindedness, which may have no more serious consequences at the breakfast table than for a man to look up and ask his wife "What did you say, dear?" may make him forget to give proper hand signals as he drives to work, with cars crowding close behind. A trivial quarrel lingering in his mind may dominate his thoughts at the moment a child runs out in the street ahead of him in pursuit of a rolling glass marble.

Long after childhood has passed, men still act on impulse. Sheer exuberance one pleasant morning may make a driver try to round a curve at a speed which hurls him off the road for good. Or, in pursuit of his own glass marble —some bit of business or golf—he will hurry along, bluffing for the right of way until he comes up against another of his own kind. Like the child running out in the path of a moving car, no driver expects trouble. It comes as a complete surprise, in a moment of impatience or inattention or unpreparedness. Or perhaps it comes when the driver, superhumanly alert and well within his rights, is struck by another driver who is superhumanly careless. It makes little difference except to a coroner's jury, whether one driver, or both, or neither was at fault. As the old epitaph puts it,

IT TAKES ONLY ONE TO MAKE AN ACCIDENT   Underwood & Underwood

"Here lies the body of William Jay
    Who died maintaining his right of way.
    Will was dead right as he sped along
    But he's just as dead as though he'd been wrong."

Human nature itself, unaided, does not make for efficient driving. Human beings, even when at the wheel, are prone to talk, wave to their friends, make love, day-dream, listen to the radio, stare at striking billboards, light cigarettes, take chances. They would not be very human if they abandoned these practices even while driving, but in the brief instant it takes to light a cigarette, many drivers' thoughts have been rudely deflated from the road into eternity.

Even when the driver is in full command of the situation, concentrating his whole attention on the highway and the problems of driving, he cannot act instantaneously. Confronted with an emergency, he jams on the brakes. Traveling at twenty miles an hour along a clear, dry road, his car requires forty-four feet to come to a stop. Its actual braking distance on that road and at that speed is twenty-two feet. What accounts for the other, possibly fatal

General Motors

THE PROVING GROUND DRIVER AND—

twenty-two? The driver is not sluggish, but he is average and human, and has a normal reaction time of three-quarters of a second. And in that fraction of a second a car going twenty miles an hour travels twenty-two feet. This fraction of a second represents the time actually consumed between the instant

Portland Cement Assn.

THE AVERAGE DRIVER HAVE THE SAME MARGIN OF SAFETY

his eyes see the danger and the moment he applies his foot to the brakes. Three-quarters of a second is an average value for this period of delay. For many drivers it is a longer interval, and for a few drivers a shorter one.

Increase the driver's speed to fifty miles an hour, a more usual rate on the open road. His reaction time does not change, but during this three-quarters-of-a-second interval a car traveling at that speed will have covered fifty-five feet, and will require a distance of almost two hundred feet to come to a stop. As the speed of the car is increased, the distance required to stop the car increases correspondingly, due to the increased distance which the car will travel during the three-quarters-of-a-second reaction-time interval, plus the increased distance required for the brakes to bring the faster-moving car to a stop after they have been applied.

Besides the general human characteristics which are common to all automobile operators, there are also individual failings which are not conducive to safe driving. A driver may have defective eyesight. One or two of every five motorists share this handicap. Worse, and very probably, he doesn't know that he has it. His limitation may take the form of being unable to see objects "out of the corner" of his eye. His field of vision may be so restricted that he sees things as though viewing them through a tunnel.

Or he may just have been drinking. No two authorities quite agree on the point at which a person who has been drinking becomes a danger, but one estimate, based on state surveys for 1937, declared that 8 per cent of all drivers and 13 per cent of all pedestrians involved in fatal accidents had been drinking. Whether these were unable to walk a straight line or speak the English language properly, or whether they merely had alcohol on their breath, is not clear. Tests made in a Milwaukee hospital show that, under the influence of alcohol, drivers' reaction time and consequent braking distance were increased by 30 per cent, that their eye and muscular coordination was 40 per cent poorer than normal, and that they made 60 per cent more errors than drivers completely sober.

The driver may have no physical ailments, but he may be a mental specimen of the type that regards the road as a sort of athletic field on which he can show off. Left unsatisfied by his humdrum daily existence, he may use highway conquests and victories over opposing cars as a means to blow up his ego.

He may be merely bull-headed, or on the other hand timid, or he may be —and very few drivers' license tests manage to discover this—definitely subnormal. In any case he is an unreliable factor to have in control of a car.

Carelessness is another human failing common to

SAFER THAN THE AVERAGE MOTORIST

Acme

many drivers. Over-confidence or boredom often produces lack of attention in an experienced driver, due to the monotony of a long or familiar trip. He may be day-dreaming when an object suddenly looms up ahead causing him to obey a reflex and become tense. If he has his foot on the accelerator, this impulse follows a pattern contrary to the muscular coordination and reflex action which are required in such a situation. It may tend not toward self-preservation but toward self-destruction. Or, finally, a driver's health may be excellent and his judgment clear, when suddenly he is faced with a complex road emergency that transcends all his experience. He is holding a hurtling instrument in his hands. Quick action and lightning precision are demanded of him. Yet something inside him clamps down—he freezes, helpless. It is—panic.

Today's driver is the same unpredictable fellow he was in the days of the Chalmers. The automobile may have dispensed with the whipstock which appeared on early models, but drivers have not rid themselves of impulses which have been part of them from time immemorial. True, training by continual automobile driving is perhaps quickening the reaction time of man as a species, but these reactions of his cannot be depended upon. Man is not a machine and he cannot be geared to function automatically as part of any machine.

Cities and states have tried to keep the driver up to date by means of legislation. They have commanded him to overcome his known limitations and to drive with robot-like precision. When he sets off from Jacksonville along the 350 miles to Miami, he is confronted with 6,760 signs on the way, telling him what to do and what not to do. They remind him of Prohibition. He becomes irritated at the heckling, moralizing free advice. He feels little guilt in evading them when he can. Each time he crosses a state line he becomes subject to a new, often unfamiliar and conflicting set of commandments. In this way, conditions are created when even an upright citizen becomes a law breaker. Signs drill into his eyes the one injunction: "Drive slowly." He is not fooled. He knows that this is a complete contradiction. Cars are built for safe, fast transportation. Although he may be unfamiliar with President Cleveland's graceful phrase about letting the law "pass into innocuous desuetude," he treats it with the same respect as another law still on the statute books: "It is not permitted in New York City to open an umbrella in the presence of a horse."

Most traffic control seems merely to try to restrict man's inalienable right to be killed at street crossings, not to aid him constructively in the pursuit of motoring happiness. It regards the motorist as a rugged individualist on whom certain checks and balances must be imposed in the form of red lights and police whistles. The control measures have been designed only to meet certain given situations, leaving many accidents within the law. For instance, in spite of the safety command to "go slow," 90 per cent of all accidents occur at comparatively low speeds. And in spite of all the rules on what to do and what not to do, nine out of ten accidents are caused, not by a mechanical failure, but by human failure.

The inference seems clear: as long as there is opportunity to make a mistake, some driver will make it. As long as there are roads on which emergencies can arise, just so long will there be drivers who fail to meet them. The present-day trend as to how to remove the risk due to the human factor is to restrict the driver. Everything is leaning toward greater restrictions as to who may drive a car, the speed at which a car may be driven, and other considerations of that nature. Authorities are trying to give more severe examinations to the driver, to make sure that only "good men" will be selected. But more severe drivers' examinations cannot produce much greater road safety. Examinations never reveal anything. Even if only the best 10 per cent of drivers were allowed to drive there would still be accidents, because this 10 per cent would at some time or other be less able to drive than it was at the time when it was tested. Tests can only reveal how an individual acts and thinks at a given moment under special circumstances—not how he acts and thinks day in and day out under a variety of different situations. In short, more severe examinations will not solve the problem. Legislating against the driver will not improve his inherent characteristics. Restricting speed is not going to solve the problem. Variable factors in the human being cannot be regulated.

It is ridiculous, for example, to pass a law saying that when one driver meets another car he must dim his lights, when this action can be achieved by mechanical means independent of the driver. The use of automatically controlled light which keeps the oncoming glare from the driver's eyes is one way of achieving the desired effect—and there are no buttons which someone must remember to push. A mechanical solution is bound to be more satisfactory than a psychological or legal solution because it regulates not only those drivers who are cooperative, intelligent and law-abiding, but all drivers.

Other forms of transportation have done a great deal in eliminating the human factor. Railroads have developed the automatic block system in which the railway track is divided into "blocks" or sections. The rails are wired so that as the wheels of one train pass over electrical contact points, the presence

RAILWAY ENGINEERS CAN'T MAKE MISTAKES   New York Central Railroad

of a train within that block is automatically signaled to the next block. Should
a second train enter the next block while the first train occupies the block
ahead, the second train would receive a "caution" signal. If the second train
passes through its block before the first train has passed out of that block, the
second train may be automatically stopped. Upon the first train advancing to
another block, a "clear" signal flashes for the second train, indicating that it is
now safe to proceed.

The locomotive engineer is not likely to make a mistake as a result of wrong
judgment. Neither is there danger of accident due to sudden absent-mindedness or physical failure. A device known as the "dead man's stick" automatically brings a train to a safe halt if the engineer's hand falls from the controls.
An efficient system of automatic signals keeps him thoroughly acquainted
with the situation ahead of him, informs him of emergencies which are not
visible to the human eye.

Present-day lack of automobile safety control cannot be excused on the grounds that the automotive industry is younger than the railroad, because the youngest of all transport facilities, the air line, also uses a number of mechanical safety devices. Airplanes utilize the radio beam and plane-to-plane and plane-to-field radio telephone. These controlling devices have one thing in common, the conjunctive operation of the right of way and vehicle. Yet even with these automatic devices, train engineers and air pilots are still carefully selected and trained for their jobs.

Travel by automobile is more than twenty-five times as great as by train, and more than seven hundred and fifty times as great as by air. Yet it is only the trains and airplanes that carry mechanical controls to provide automatic aid for their drivers. Radio beams, block systems and other devices could be applied to the automobile, not exactly, but in general principle.

In the motor car itself much has been done in the last twenty years. The phenomenal·nature of these advances makes one think that the advances in the next twenty years will be even quicker and greater than anything that has been done so far. The engine may be moved from the present location to a place under the floor or in the rear, giving many improvements, including improved vision and the possibility of building a more resilient and safe bumper at the front of the car. It will have a higher speed and it will be used at that speed. No driver always drives at full speed, but he will use that speed as freely on the proper roads as he now uses twenty-five at best on a crowded highway. Tires will be made resistant to the effects of heat, oil and gasoline so that they can withstand the higher speeds of twenty years from now as they withstand the present-day driving speed. Cars will be smaller but roomier. Interiors will be more flexible as to use. They will be air conditioned. Cars will be more comfortable to ride in, more economical to run, and capable of higher speed. But none of these improvements will mean a thing if there is not a corresponding advance in safety. Given a 1960 automobile, with its

[55]

Portland Cement Assn.   ONE PLUS ONE MAKES TWO BUT TWO PLUS TWO MAKES THREE   Ge1

tremendous technical advances and capabilities, the 1940 driver would probably find it simply a more economical and quicker way to get himself into
a smash-up.

But with the changes in the car, will the driver too be changed? Will he
have lost one bad trait which made him years ago a menace to his own safety
and a nuisance to others? Don't count on it. But these cars of 1960 and the
highways on which they drive will have in them devices which will correct
the faults of human beings as drivers. They will prevent the driver from com-
mitting errors. They will prevent his turning out into traffic except when he
should. They will aid him in passing through intersections without slowing
down or causing anyone else to do so and without endangering himself or
others. Many present beginnings give hints of the kind of over-all planning
on which the near future could realize. Everything will be designed by engineering, not by legislation, not in piecemeal fashion, but as a complete job. The
two, the car and the road, are both essential to the realization of automatic
safety. It is a job that must be done by motor-car manufacturers and road
builders cooperatively. Such devices when adopted will not be included in
just this car or that. They would do no good just here and there. They will
be obligatory for all cars. They will prevent a car from turning out of a lane
except under favorable circumstances. They will prevent him from moving

AUTOMATIC CAR CONTROL WOULD AID THE SAFE DRIVER AND CURB THE BAD DRIVER

from one highway artery into another until his speed has been brought up or down to the rate of the new artery he is to enter. They will safeguard traffic lanes from right or left interference. They will make it possible for him to proceed at full speed through dense fog. They will aid him as he travels at night, as he crosses mountain ranges, as he traverses the breadth of the country and as he drives through city streets.

In 1940 many people felt that those drivers who blundered ought to be driven off the highway. But since almost everyone at some time blundered— indeed, couldn't help blundering, given such a set-up of unworkable laws and obsolete roads—that demand was much too difficult ever to be carried out. It usually worked out in the sense that the blunderers drove themselves off the highways—into the ditch. But in 1960 they all stay out of the ditch. It is not done by law, but through the very nature of the car and the highway. They still blunder, of course, but when they do, they are harmless.

SEPARATED LANES OF TRAFFIC

Have you ever conceived of a road which would allow no car to approach your own—which would hold you to your course without the danger of being struck or of striking any object—where you could decide in advance how fast you would like to drive, and by maintaining that constant, effortless pace, arrive at your destination on scheduled time? It sounds impossible? But you can have such a road. The means of bringing it about are available. The idea is thoroughly practical. It can be built to work in conjunction with an automatic control installed in your car. The highway you use can be made as safe and pleasant at all times as it would be if your car were the only automobile upon it.

Today, in the course of an average mile drive through traffic, your automobile is exposed to several hundred cars, moving in every direction and at every variation in speed from ten to seventy miles an hour. In this disorderly traffic flow, there can be no certainty that one car of all those hundreds will not meet you head-on, crash in behind you or suddenly lash against the side of your car. It is not only the accident, but the fear of accident, which retards

TRAFFIC TUNED TO THE TEMPO OF GENTLER TIMES   Henry Flan

NEW YORK CITY TRAFFIC CONTROL   Margaret Bourke-White   SOFT SHOULDERS   Portland Cement Assn.

the effective use of the motor car. Wherever there is danger, traffic is forced to go slowly, which causes delay, congestion, exasperated drivers, more accidents. The highway attributes that produce accidents are four in number. They are known to everyone.

First: The crossroad. Here two crossing streams of traffic using the same pavement cause the greatest congestion on the highway today. This problem will be discussed in the next chapter.

Second: The road edge. Stationary hazards at the roadside, such as soft shoulders, culverts, fences, hydrants, telephone poles, parked cars, as well as moving objects, such as jay-walkers or stray dogs wandering onto the highway, cause motorists to crowd inward away from them and thus slow down traffic.

Third: Cars moving in opposite directions. This with its head-on collisions results in more fatal accidents than any other type.

Fourth: Cars moving in the same direction but at different speeds. This is an important cause of retardation of traffic flow and is the greatest cause of automobile accidents. It results in rear-end collisions and the sideswiping of two cars in adjacent lanes.

HEAD-ON HAZARD   Portland Cement Assn.   THREE SPEEDS AHEAD   Ewing Galloway

Dr. Miller McClintock, Director of the Yale University Bureau for Street Traffic Research, who devised the audit count which has become the basis of many American city traffic patterns, has aptly expressed these four factors which retard the smooth flow of traffic in the following terms:

At crossroads: intersectional friction.

At the road edge: marginal friction.

Between cars moving in opposite directions: medial friction.

Between cars moving in the same direction: internal-stream friction.

When cars could travel at only ten miles an hour, it was not a serious inconvenience if they held each other up. But when they can travel at present-day speeds, it is serious, unfair, uneconomical and dangerous. It is only now—when speed is here to stay—that it has become necessary to correct the various kinds of interference.

Prior to the automobile era, when animal-drawn carts and foot traffic traveling on single-lane dirt roads met another vehicle traveling in the opposite direction, each pulled half way off the road to facilitate passing. With the introduction of the automobile, due to the faster speeds involved, a different type of right of way was demanded, a highway permitting clear travel in two directions simultaneously. The simplest type of such a road is two lanes in opposite directions. On a two-lane road one car overtaking another traveling in the same direction is expected to pass by pulling over into the lane of opposing traffic. This was adequate at first, when there were few cars, but today at modern road speeds, the intrusion of an automobile moving in one direction into a line of cars moving in another direction is a matter of life or death. In spite of

98% OF U. S. ROADS INVITE THE HEAD-ON

Portland Cement Assn.

this peril, many state highways in the United States are still only two lanes wide—not just a great number or large majority, but by actual count 98 per cent.

Where traffic is heavy, the general practice has been to add more lanes. The unhappy fact is that

ADDING LANES MULTIPLIES ACCIDENTS

the mere widening of roads tends to promote accidents rather than prevent them. Traffic studies indicate that for an equal number of miles traveled there are only three accidents on a two-lane road to every four accidents on the wider highways. Three-lane highways, where cars fly at each other like game cocks battling for use of the center lane, are particularly tempting for head-on collisions. To eliminate this danger, on highways widened to four and six lanes physical separation of opposing streams of traffic is a recent development. Such two-way divided roads are an obvious improvement over the three-lane undivided roads. But such physical division is the exception rather than the rule, and in its absence, the accident rate increases as the number of lanes is increased. Mid-road collisions cause nearly one-fifth of all accidents on the highway. Four years ago, Mr. H. C. Dickinson of the National Bureau of Standards said: "We should never have built, and should stop building now, main country thoroughfares carrying heavy traffic in both directions on the same pavement."

Segregating opposing streams of traffic by means of the one-way street is common practice. Nor is it a modern idea. The Romans did it. Today this

[65]

venerable practice survives and still proves its worth. Studies made on Chestnut, Walnut and Market Streets in Philadelphia, before and after their conversion to one-way arteries, show that speed is increased by more than 20 per cent, that traffic volume is increased by more than 20 per cent, and that accidents between intersections have been materially reduced.

Through the countryside, one-way roads would be equally desirable, but they cannot be achieved as simply as one-way streets within a city. Closely parallel routes with frequent interconnections are limited to the cities, and the arbitrary conversion of country roads into one-way traffic channels would work a hardship on local traffic.

The first step toward separating streams of traffic on the existing rural highways was taken in 1911, after Edward Hines, Road Commissioner of Wayne County, Michigan, saw an automobile almost collide with a horse and buggy on a narrow bridge. Realizing that neither driver involved could do more than make a guess as to where the exact center of the road lay, Mr. Hines ordered white lines painted down the middle of every bridge and curve under his authority. Later he extended these lines along the full length of his paved roads. That was nearly thirty years ago. Today an assortment of solid lines, double lines, dotted lines,

Above: SAFETY THROUGH RAISED ARROWS
Below: SAFETY THROUGH PAINT ROUGH GOING FOR TRESPASSERS

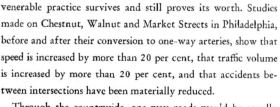

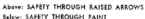

Acme
Portland Cement Assn.

dashes and arrows, painted white, yellow or black divide the highways. This practice marks an advance in safety, but it is not a guarantee. Good drivers like to know where the middle of the road is, in order to stay away from it. But bad drivers, the road hog, the novice, the drunk, the show-off, and all that reckless tribe, are inclined to straddle the mark. Some, with a phobia against the road's edge, hug the line so closely that they sideswipe cars to the left of them.

The neutral strip used for central division on wider roadways is in effect a mere broadening of the painted line. From three and a half to four feet in width, such a strip is frequently laid in contrasting colors of material to differentiate it from that part of the road devoted to traffic lanes.

Lanes themselves have also been laid down in contrasting road surfaces. "Psychology" road design has been tried on the highway between Richmond and Petersburg, Virginia; in Rhode Island on the Putnam Pike, Gooseneck Hill Road; on the Boston Post Road and others. On these four-lane roads, light-colored smooth cement lanes have been built on either side of a central paving of coarse-textured black macadam. The macadam is wide enough for two additional lanes and a three-foot neutral strip which is marked off by white lines. No one wants to hear the roar of his tires over the rough-surfaced macadam for an appreciable distance if he can help it, so drivers keep away from the center of the road except when passing. There were twenty-seven accidents on the Putnam Pike in 1936, before the center of the road was rough-paved, and only eight accidents in the year afterwards.

On many California roads, arrow-shaped protuberances have been set in a line along the middle of the road, not sufficiently high to present a hazard but making continuous driving in the center of the road dis-

Above: SAFETY THROUGH PSYCHOLOGY
Below: BARS FOR INSOMNIA

tinctly uncomfortable. A similar drastic inducement to keep the center strip free for emergencies is a series of raised domes. These devices undoubtedly serve a safety purpose, but it is a curious paradox that road builders should deliberately design discomfort into heavily traveled highways.

Still another type of central divider, which takes up no more space than the painted line already used for marking off one-way traffic, has been tried on Ramona Boulevard in Los Angeles. Convex metal bands mounted on steel springs at the height of a hub-cap had already proved strong and resilient when used as roadside guard rails. Two such convex metal bands mounted on steel springs were bolted back to back and mounted on steel posts in the center of the Boulevard, making it impossible for cars to cross over onto the opposing lanes. Near Lansing, Michigan, a strip of corrugated steel has been laid down the center of the road, with slanting grooves so designed that they grip the wheels of an encroaching car and turn it back onto its lane of the highway.

Devices of this type are possible, however, only on wide roadways with room for at least two lanes on each side of the road, so that no car need ever cross over into opposing streams of traffic. And they do not prevent a car that is out of control from crashing across the road.

On a few thoroughfares there has been one masterly

E. Donald Sterner, New Jersey Highway Commissioner

TRAFFIC SEPARATION REDUCES
DEATH FOUR-FIFTHS

[68]

CARELESS DRIVING HERE GETS A BATH

improvement in design. It is the first real step toward motorways on which cars can move in safety at the speed for which they were built. On about one-fifth of the 3,303 miles of four- and six-lane roads in our state highway systems, the road is now divided by something more effective than painted lines and bumpy arrows. Raised islands have been introduced on many roads which provide a real barrier between streams of opposing traffic. Highways with central division of this sort were first tried out around large cities, notably Detroit, in 1925. As late as 1931, they were not widely favored by highway engineers, but now they are generally considered to have proven their worth, despite the fact that their average cost is a third greater than that of the undivided four-lane highway. In a mile-long stretch of highway on Chicago's Outer Drive, where this type of division is used, the fatal accident rate for four years has been only one in every forty million vehicle miles, which is one-fifth the accident rate of the nation as a whole.

The central division of two-way thoroughfares, then, varies all the way from the painted line to wide parkways planted with shrubbery to screen off one side of the road from the other. The best central parkway divisions have low, sloping arched curbs, tending to slow down cars which are forced off the

[69]

roadway by any emergency, and thus making it easier to stop them safely.

The outside edge of the road presents dangers that must also be eliminated. One of the earliest devices used to prevent vehicles from encroaching on pedestrian walkways is the simple curb. But as a roadside guard for motor traffic, it is too rigid and unyielding. More resilient roadside guards have long been employed along curves and embankments, and have proved more effective in holding cars on the road. Convex metal bands and steel cable strung between concrete posts are in common use. Wide grass strips along the right of way of many new boulevards provide safety for a car forced off the road surface by an emergency, and enable it to park without blocking the lane.

There are other elements of traffic which must be separated too. It is not enough just to separate traffic moving in opposite directions. To prevent cars weaving from lane to lane and to eliminate sideswiping, lanes of cars moving in the same direction must be divided one from another. Separators which require an appreciable amount of road space are unsuited to segregating individual lanes. Experiments have been conducted with many types that are sufficiently compact to be practical for lane division.

Four or five years ago, ruts were built into the Queensboro Bridge in New York City, but they were so ineptly designed that the experiment was abandoned after a few days. The fault was one of design—the spacing between ruts was wrong, so that considerable damage was done to tires, and the width of the ruts was too close to tire width so that unless the driver was practiced at driving in these particular ruts he continually burned the sidewall of one tire or another. Raised portions along the center part of the lane, which the car must straddle, have been tried, too, in an attempt to keep cars in a particular lane. These humps, ruts or rails are attempts to provide for the automobile tracks which are as restricting as railroad tracks are to the train. They are experimental types and not always successful, but at least they point in the

HORSE SENSE BUILT THIS NATURAL SIDE BARRIER

right direction, toward methods of segregating individual lanes of traffic.

A more practical solution to this problem might be found just by looking at the simplest of our roads. People who have lived on the land will remember that on dirt roads which had been worn down below the level of the fields by travel it was difficult for even a runaway horse to crash with its buggy into a rail fence up above. The chance angle of roadside slope would automatically turn the buggy's wheels back onto the road. If something desirable can happen by chance, why shouldn't it be made to function even better by design? Suppose that the edge of a modern concrete highway did not stop, as it often does, in a declivity or soft shoulder, but was curved up at either side. Any car out of control would be automatically turned back onto the road, if the curve were properly designed. The upward curving edge of the road itself could effectively serve both as safety device and separator.

Many devices of this sort have been patented. Some separators are designed in the form of a wave crest, running along the sides of the road. As a runaway car climbs up toward the under side of the wave's crest, its wheels are deflected back onto the straight course. This type of separator could be built of steel mesh woven

METAL ADAPTATION OF
SIDE BARRIER

[71]

in basket-weave fashion. It could be made of concrete, built as part of the road itself. It could be of prefabricated sheet-metal construction. More flexible materials would lessen the shock in turning the car back to its channel.

Separators can prevent sideswiping and head-on accidents, but as long as there are cars moving at different speeds in the same lane of traffic there will be delay and the danger of rear-end collision. Attempts have been made to separate passenger cars from trucks by forbidding the heavier vehicles to use certain highways; but this does not make for a larger and more efficient use of our roadways. The motor truck and the motor car are capable of maintaining comparable speed, and as long as a truck can move fast enough to keep out of the way of the car behind it, there seems to be no more valid reason for separating it from the passenger car than there would be for separating red cars from blue ones. The traffic problem will not be solved by setting aside one road for larger vehicles and another for small ones. All that need be expected of any motor vehicle using the highway is that it stay out of the way of other cars. This involves a question of speed, not of size.

In a large percentage of accidents, high speed is not the primary factor, though it may greatly increase their intensity. In the last eleven years, the maximum speeds at which passenger cars can travel have been increased by 50 per cent, and there is no indication that a top limit has been approached. Permissible speeds on the highways lag far behind the effective speed of a car. Disregarding the question of highway intersection, the subject discussed in the next chapter, if cars could be kept apart, traveling in each lane at uniform speeds, with physical separation between the lanes and automatic control between cars to provide equal spacing, cars could travel with safety at much greater speeds than they do today. Although many states have established maximum speed limits, and twenty-two states have legislation concerning driving at unreasonably low speeds, few attempts have been made to fix definitely the speed of automobiles on any given highway or in any particular lane of any highway. To be effective such restrictions must be absolute, and they should not be enforced by law, but automatically. Legislation which permits the driver to apply his own initiative could not be made sufficiently rigid.

Automatic controls have already been provided to govern certain factors of traffic operation. The most common of these is perhaps the automatic traffic-light system. And it is not a much greater engineering undertaking to develop controls which can be made to provide definite speed standardization on the highway. Photo-electric traffic traps are individual means used today for measuring traffic speed, which is merely the first step toward control. William A. Halstead is developing a small short-range radio broadcasting unit which has as its primary purpose the instruction of traffic. This unit located along the highway can broadcast messages to motorists through their standard car radio equipment for the particular section of the highway covered by the transmitter station. The transmitter repeats the traffic bulletins automatically, and these bulletins may be instantly changed at the transmitter or by telephone from a central traffic station. Experiments are being conducted with a cable along the highway, from which messages emanate. The same mechanism could transmit visual traffic light signals directly to miniature signal lights within the car. Further developments of this system along the lines of car-to-car radio hook-up might be used to advise a driver nearing an intersection of the approach of another car or even to maintain control of speed and spacing of cars in the same traffic lane.

In essentials, the methods of controlling traffic which have been described here provide for a restricted right of way in the form of individual traffic lanes, and for the standardization of the speeds of cars within each of these lanes. Here we have a direct comparison to the railroad. The tracks provide definite control as to the path which a train must follow, and the railroad signal block system controls spacing between trains on the same track or traffic lane. These devices could be applied directly to the control of automobile traffic. A road surface constructed with grooves in which the car would be guided would prevent the car from deviating from its fixed lane of travel. Also, the highway could be divided into signal blocks acting to prevent the cars from encroaching upon one another. However, applying such control means to automobile traffic becomes too restrictive and prevents the full utilization of the benefits of the automobile which come from the car's flexibility. Nor is such a control system applicable to the characteristic operations of the automobile.

Within the field of science there are many potential devices which could be developed to fit exactly the needs of traffic control as they have been defined here. One of these, for instance, the radio beam, is now being used in a limited form for the guiding of the airplane on its course. The field of electromagnetic emanations, which cover a very wide field of electric-wave impulses, is probably the best adapted to the control of traffic. It is conceivable that a

PLANE PILOT GETS DOT DASH OR DASH DOT SIGNAL IF NOT ON COURSE. ALONG THE BLACK LINE
SIGNALS COMBINE TO CAUSE A STEADY HUM
United Airlines

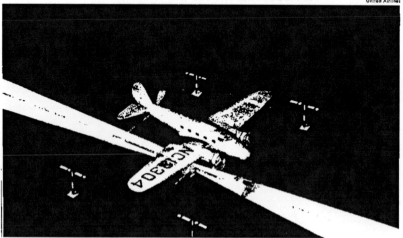

control operating directly —as a radio beam, broadcast from stations located along the highway— could provide the control desired. Or perhaps more simply, an electrical conductor imbedded within the road surface, carrying an electric current producing an electro-magnetic field, might provide direct control.

Having provided a control medium, whatever its form, it is logical to expect that this medium

ONE MAN GUIDES HUNDREDS OF TRAINS SAFELY

could be applied to control both the speed of the car and its path of travel. A constant prescribed speed on the highway can be maintained by causing the impulses to accelerate or decelerate the car engine. By the same method the interval between cars can be set and controlled. The interval would be set to conform with the safe stopping distance necessary for the speed of the car. The individual instructions for each car would be transmitted over the control axis. Therefore, we have within one control medium the ability to maintain these cars within a lane and to maintain them at a uniform standardized speed. Also it would not be necessary to widen highways to set up this type of invisible separator and control, as it would be with physical separators. This automatic control of a car could not be put into the car alone or into the

[75]

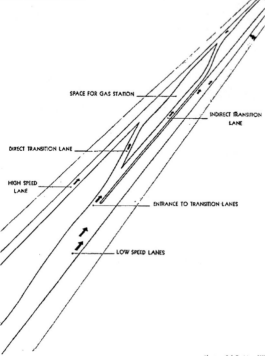

SPACE FOR GAS STATION

INDIRECT TRANSITION LANE

DIRECT TRANSITION LANE

HIGH SPEED LANE

ENTRANCE TO TRANSITION LANES

LOW SPEED LANES

Norman Bel Geddes, 1935
TRANSITION FROM ONE SPEED TO ANOTHER—TOMORROW

highway. alone. The major part will be in the car, but its complementary elements must be in the highway.

Whether lanes of traffic are segregated by physical separators or by some type of automatic mechanism, lanes within the highway will be designed to permit traffic operation at specified, controlled speeds. In the case of multi-lane highways, it is conceivable that a certain lane may be designed for high-speed travel and other lanes for a lower speed. All the advanced features of highway design will be incorporated in the multi-lane motorways. Separate strips of motorway will be constructed for traffic flowing at different specific speeds.

The automatically controlled motorway will provide for low, medium and high speeds, and those speeds will be mechanically enforced so that there will be no variation from them. Separate lanes within these strips will allow traffic to move at controlled speeds. When you drive, you choose your lane according to how fast you want to go, and the speed is automatically maintained as long as you are in that lane. The miles fly by under your wheels. Nothing

[76]

short of an unforeseen emergency will permit you to slow down. No chicken or pedestrian can stray in from the roadside. The motorway is designed exclusively for the motorist. Others will be kept off by physical barriers, and physical or electro-magnetic separators hold you to a carefree, undeviating course down the center of your lane.

When you desire to drive in a faster or slower speed lane, a means is provided for transferring from one speed to another. At transition points, located at regular intervals on the motorway, the grass space between groups of speed lanes is broadened out. In this space is a single-lane cross-over channel that permits a gradual approach from one speed lane to another. It is long enough to allow your car to accelerate or decelerate to the speed of the lane to which you are changing. Before the transition point is reached, you press a button on your instrument panel, indicating that you want to turn left or right into the next lane, just as today you press a button on your radio to tune in on a station of a particular wave length. When your car reaches the entrance to the cross-over channel, the controlling device in your car picks up and is guided by the controlling forces from the cross-over channel, switching the car from the straight-through lane into this channel. Once on this lane, the control gradually brings you to the speed of the new lane in which you are to travel. Similarly your car is switched into the new lane at the junction between it and the cross-over.

Temporarily there may be no space available on that lane because of traffic density. When such a condition exists, your car, starting to travel on the cross-over, is switched into a lane running between the two groups

[77]

TRANSITION FROM ONE SPEED TO ANOTHER—TODAY

MULTI-DECK MOTORWAYS COULD USE THE TOP OF A GREAT POWER DAM

of speed lanes and parallel to them. On this you slow down or stop, until receiving a "clear" signal, then accelerate and enter the higher- or lower-speed traffic lane. Any delay encountered occasionally at a point like this is more than compensated for by the steady, even pace you are able to maintain once you are in your desired speed lane. And, of course, there may be no delay at all. If the lane is clear, you enter the new lane without stopping.

Whether you are shifting from low speed to medium, medium to high, or from the higher speeds to the lower, this same procedure is followed. And as you enter a lane, you never have to jam frantically on your brakes, fearing that as you emerge into the traffic stream a car may come hurtling at you. When the automatic controls allow you to make the shift, you make it with perfect safety. Once in the lane, cars move ahead, behind and on either side of you, but automatic lane separation and spacing make it impossible for another car to collide with you, sideswipe you or cut in ahead of you. Car-to-car or station-to-car control keeps the automobile behind you at its proper distance. You do not need to use your horn (with which your car is equipped for local roads) on *this* motorway, because you never have to pass a car. You cannot go faster. The car ahead of you cannot slow down. The car in front moves on at the same speed as your own because both cars are traveling at the automatically prescribed speed within that lane. Before you the road is always clear, as far as you need to use it.

At regular intervals along the motorway there are traffic control stations. These may be located about five miles apart. The officers in each tower have complete authority over the section of road two and a half miles on either side of them. From their vantage point they can see the traffic flowing past them, and with their instruments they can communicate with any car in the territory under their jurisdiction.

Suppose that on this motorway you run out of gas or have engine failure

CONTROL BRIDGE: OCEAN LINER STYLE

Kurt Sch

CONTROL BRIDGE: FUTURE MOTORWAY STYLE

or a pump leak. A slowing down or stopped car automatically notifies the
two nearest traffic control towers. From either control tower the stopped car
could probably be seen. It is within two and a half miles of one or the other
tower. It takes the cars in front of you about six minutes to clear the two and
a half miles. Cars behind the stopped car would be turned off into other
lanes of traffic if adjacent lanes were not at capacity. An emergency car from

[81]

the control tower would immediately speed down the new open lane and would remove your car from traffic. Stoppage of traffic in this lane would affect a minimum of cars for a maximum of ten minutes. No glass would be shattered, no cars crumpled, no blood shed, no lives taken.

A motorway of this type, permitting constant high speeds, lies in the near future. But the ability to travel in this manner already lies in your car today. It is simply that disorderly, congested traffic on roads originally designed for wagons prevents the car from utilizing its potentialities. But functional road design will cure this situation.

EVERY HIGHWAY INTERSECTION IS OBSOLETE

I F A psychiatrist were set to work examining all the occupational neuroses of the motorist, it might take him years to do the cataloguing. But any driver can investigate his own lost temper, jagged nerves and week-end nightmares. Just put him on the open road and he will give his diagnosis without further delay. Wiping his brow he will admit that the cause is not complex or far to seek; its name is simply "frustration."

The old phrase, "the open road," always had a pleasant connotation. In earlier days the roads bore so little traffic that they were really open. There were no cars at a standstill wherever roads met. The meeting of hay wagons at the crossing of two farm roads was not a serious traffic condition. They were not moving fast enough. With the advent of the automobile, however, a real problem was created and the solution to this problem is a real necessity in this day of increasing traffic volume. There are many conditions under which different roads meet, each of them creating a separate problem; but essentially the conditions fall into two categories—the junction and the intersection.

JUNCTION   Gendreau

A junction occurs when two roads or lanes come together without crossing one another. The shape of such junctions may take the form of a T when roads join at right angles, or may form a Y if they join at an acute angle. Both types are extremely common along highways today. They offer no great problem of solution if one of the roads carries traffic in one direction only, thus avoiding left-hand turns across traffic. But when traffic moves in two directions on both roads, it is a very serious problem. For complete flexibility of traffic movement in such a case, left-hand turns must be permitted. Under present highway design practice this can only be accomplished satisfactorily with traffic lights.

The first problem which the average motorist runs into every day is right at his own driveway, at the junction where the driveway meets the street forcing him to make a right-angled turn. He wants to turn into the street, but he is blocked off by traffic there. He gets off to a slow start. When he gets an opening, he swings out into the flow of traffic, at once becoming an obstruction at his slower speed, due to the small radius of the turn.

When two or more roads or streams of traffic come together and cross each other an intersection is created. Here the driver has all the difficulties of a junction—cars turning into each others' paths—plus the difficulties of cars crossing each others' paths. The simple definition of an intersection conceals the confusion that may result when at some city square or circle a half dozen traffic channels, of different sizes and densities, aim at each other from all around the compass. The intersection is the chief stumbling block for high-

FREE-FOR-ALL INTERSECTION

way designers and the chief headache for the traffic police. It is
inherently the most heavily used point on the highway. Those
standards of safety, comfort, speed and economy do not find
very eloquent expression at that point. Every major intersection
is a scene of contest or conflict—usually supervised by an umpire
in the form of a traffic light, assisted by one or more traffic
officers.

The conventional cross-shaped intersection served its purpose
when conveyances were light and traffic was sparse. The old
mud-and-dust buggy crossing, although a relic of the past, may
until recently have met all needs. There are still back roads where
that crossing is adequate if a driver can look out for the other
car over a wide stretch of fields. The chance of collision in thinly
populated open country is remote. Even if the automobile driver
slows down, his loss of time is slight, and it is not multiplied out
of all reason by the resulting delay to hundreds of cars behind
him. This same driver will lose more time and run more risks at
intersecting streets and well-paved highways guarded by traffic
lights than he will where wagon roads cross in the fields.

Why should the crossroads most heavily traveled today be the
ones that are least adapted to the safe flow of the vehicles that
use them? The average car weighs about a ton and a half. At
sixty miles an hour a car would strike a stationary object with
as much force as if it had been dropped from a twelve-story
building, and the chance that you may strike or be struck by one
of them as you cross a highway checks your speed at every intersection.

The intersection problem is complicated by the fact that it

Camera Guild

BAD ROADS ARE NOT SO BAD
WHEN YOU SEE YOUR
NEIGHBOR COMING

[87]

tangles many kinds of traffic. It tangles pedestrian traffic, livestock, slow cars, fast cars—which because of their half dozen inherent different speeds cause confusion and breakdown of the optimum speed. Over and beyond that there are the many street corners that have their own particular human factor in the shape of the traffic cop and his privileges. The cop too often exercises his own idea of traffic control rather than enforcing a predetermined plan. Street corners have their own quota of signs bearing directions, instructions and warnings. At railroad grade-crossings, sign language has been particularly prevalent. The driver approaches the danger-spot—often hidden behind a curve—keeping his eye on the road. At the same moment a suspended sign tells him to "stop, look and listen." But he can't keep his eye on the road and on the signs too. The universal American stop sign has a fatal tendency to appear so frequently that it is ignored. Surveys have shown that six drivers out of every ten drive past them without making a stop. Yet, the signs are the first line of defense of right-angled grade crossings.

SIX OUT OF TEN DON'T   Camera Guild

This type of intersection occurs on three-fourths of all the occasions when two American thoroughfares meet. If you put up a traffic sign you are putting your trust in the driver's proper functioning, his willingness to cooperate, his individual sense of caution. These are risky, unstable factors to rely upon. Large signs, clanging bells, watchmen waving flags, and gates barring the way are just a few of the most common devices which have been tried at railroad crossings to abolish accidents. Intersections should be designed so that instead of requesting safety, they guarantee it.

Human factors at railroad crossings, even when given these aids, are described in many national statistics. A single example may be just as dramatic. A study made by the Erie Railroad of the total number of grade-crossing accidents along its lines in 1937 showed:

Acme

AND TWENTY-TWO PER CENT LOSE

in 6 per cent of the cases the cars crashed through the lowered bars and then collided with a train; in 20 per cent, the watchman's stop signs were ignored; in 22 per cent the automobiles ran into the side of the train. Nearly 70 per cent of these accidents occurred at grade crossings protected by flashers, gates or watchmen and in nearly 30 per cent of the cases, cars stalled in front of the train.

Motorists and railroad authorities are aware of the element of peril accompanying the human factor. For years there has been agitation, in small townships as well as in state legislatures, to eliminate railroad grade crossings.

About 2000 over- or underpasses are built each year. But that figure pales into insignificance when one learns that over 230,-000 primitive grade crossings still remain. This is an average of about one

"WHEN SHALL WE THREE MEET AGAIN?"

grade crossing for each mile of railroad in the country.

The practice of delaying half the traffic to give the other half a right of way goes back to the earliest days of the railroad. The first railroads improved upon the pace of horse-drawn traffic but did not improve on its intersection design. The result was train wrecks. To curb the incidence of murder at crossings, a Kansas legislator drafted the following bill, and helped to have it enacted: "When two trains meet at an intersection both shall come to a full stop, and neither shall proceed until the other gets out of the way."

More than half of all intersection accidents between two automobiles occur at right-angled crossings. At in intersection, the driver usually has two choices: to lose time but play safe by stopping before the intersection, or to save time but take a chance by going ahead. A fast-moving vehicle on a straight stretch of highway driven by a good driver with a better than average reaction time requires a certain stopping distance when an obstacle appears in its path. At an intersection there is a further complication, because the driver now sees approaching at a right angle another vehicle whose speed he must estimate. He must be sure that his car and the other one will not meet at the intersection at the same minute and he must be sure of that fact at a distance from the intersection not only dependent on his speed but the estimated speed of the opposing car. What is even more vital is this: if he does make up his mind, and the other driver also makes up his mind, are they going to agree? It is a worse gamble than throwing dice. At least in dice one of the players is sure to win.

The last few years have seen many ingenious attempts to coax surer responses out of the consciousness of the driver as he hurtles, innocently or absently, toward an intersection. In California, the approach to certain intersections has been made intentionally bumpy, to joggle fast drivers into slowing down before they reach the crossing. The cluster of bumps on the road before an intersection wakes up and warns the sleepy or absent-minded driver. Another idea is a pressed diamond pattern in the concrete at intersectional approaches. The rush of the driver's tires over the pattern gives off a loud hum, distinct from the sound of the smooth-surfaced road with a clear right of way, and thus serves as a reminder.

But the universal deterrent is still the traffic light. In its usual form it switches on and off, red to green, with no more than a theoretical regard for the volume of traffic actually moving or halting before it. It calls on the motorist for patience, submission and a waste of time, gas and nerves.

The Automatic Signal Corporation already has perfected a system which has reduced these nuisances. A unit buried in the road operates the traffic lights as a car passes over it. The device can be set so that the light can remain fixed for any interval desired. After that period, which may be long enough for several cars to pass through, it changes. A car running over the device immediately after this change cannot trip the signal again until a certain time has elapsed. The fixed interval is dependent on the traffic volume, the period being longer on the highway with the greatest density. Besides this system, an electro-magnetic device is in extensive use, which functions similarly, but the activating mechanism is a roller set flush in the road surface.

There have been reformers and idealists in the cause of stop-and-go lights. As early as 1916, Ernest P. Goodrich and others began to advocate the use of signals so systematized that if a motorist drove at a stipulated, uniform speed, he would find all the lights green as he approached them. Two types of this system for continuous movement of cars have been devised. In one, all lights on one street change at the same time, but these lights are grouped, say, three greens together, then three reds. The second type, a flexible progressive system, was first installed in the Chicago Loop area in 1926. Under this system, the length of time allotted to the green light is adjusted to the stipulated speed of cars approaching it and also to the length of the block down which they travel. It is considerably more expensive to install and maintain than the simpler system, but it comes nearer to providing what is necessary—a steady flow of traffic all along our highways.

Beyond such ingenious devices lie the solutions which do away with traffic lights entirely. When the driver approaches what he knows will be a busy intersection, it is a pleasant surprise, instead of having to jam on the brakes at the flash of a red light, to find himself routed upon a circular roadway from which four highways radiate. He wants to turn left, but he is deflected to the right around the traffic circle. Two cars are immediately ahead of him. He sees one of them turn out to complete a right-hand turn, and the other turn right at the half-way point to continue in the original direction before the circle was reached. His own car goes three-quarters of the way around before it completes the left turn. Only when he is out of the circle does he realize that two-directional traffic from four points of the compass went around that rotary simultaneously and no car stopped. All cars moved in the same direction, so there could be no head-on crashes. Right-angle collisions are a possibility at the junctions of the thoroughfares with the circle. However, the risk of rear-end and sideswiping complications is considerable. Progress around the rotary is slow, for all cars have to weave from lane to lane and are slowed down by the cars feeding in ahead. The rotary is not a final solution.

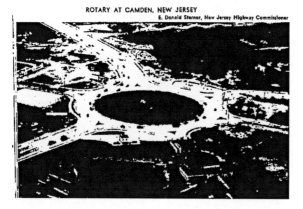

ROTARY AT CAMDEN, NEW JERSEY
E. Donald Sterner, New Jersey Highway Commissioner

Traffic circles such as these have been introduced into rural highways quite recently, but they were employed in city street design long before there was any motor traffic at all. Monument Circle in Indianapolis was designed in 1821, by Ralston, an assistant of Major L'Enfant. It is now used by as many as 2000 cars an hour, and serves as the terminal for all the city bus lines. The four smaller "islands" at the entrance to each of the four avenues radiating from the circle serve pedestrians and act to turn traffic to its proper course. The comparatively large size of the central circle is highly desirable for rotary traffic, but it is also important to have wide curves where traffic turns into the circle. In this instance, the curb radius at these corners is only fifteen feet. As the minimum turning radius of American cars varies from seventeen to twenty-six feet, none can make this turn, no matter at what speed, without edging over into the path of cars to the left.

The rotary circle located in rural highways where traffic is intermittent allows for a constant and steady flow of traffic at all times. Although such traffic may have to slow up somewhat due to the limited radius of the circle as generally built, such traffic can at least move through the intersection without danger of serious collision. If these radii were increased to the comparable speed of the traffic, slowing down would not be necessary. Also if route directions were supplied to the driver before he reached the traffic circle, much of the confusion and retardation of the traffic flow within the circle, due to the attention of the driver being diverted when looking for direction signs, would be eliminated. Traffic circles handling large volumes of traffic are very inefficient due to the weaving from lane to lane in dense traffic.

INDIANAPOLIS' FAMOUS MONUMENT DOESN'T HELP TRAFFIC
W. H. Bass

NO NEED TO STOP, LOOK, LISTEN

Constant and steady flow results only when conflicting currents of moving
traffic are really segregated. This can be obtained by overpasses and underpasses which provide a high degree of safety. The best commentary, for example, on the elimination of railroad grade crossings is that from 1928 to
1939—although the number of cars using the road has increased by over five
million—the number of fatalities at crossings has decreased by 40 per cent.
To most people overpasses and underpasses for roadways are welcome new
departures. But actually they are not so new. These ideas, along with other
very sophisticated methods of traffic control, were used over eighty years ago.

Most people who today use the segregated footpaths, bridle paths, prom-
enades, and cross-town arteries of New York's Central Park have never heard
the names Frederick Law Olmstead and Calvert Vaux. Least of all do they
realize that the park was laid out in the pre-jigsaw days of 1858, and that
Olmstead's and Vaux's designing was so sound and so prophetic that it has
never had to be subjected to major changes. Pedestrian and vehicular traffic
in Central Park are separated, to their mutual advantage. There are meander-
ing pleasure paths, but there are also straight channels for commercial traffic
to cross the park by the most direct route. Slow traffic is not endangered and
fast traffic is not impeded. One is completely segregated from the other. Olm-

stead's and Vaux's plan also provided for a uniform directional flow of traffic moving counterclockwise through the park without intersectional delay. With such a history of daring innovations, Central Park could well have become the public school for several generations of American highway engineers.

To sum up: two ideas have taken hold in modern intersectional design. First is that of the overpass or underpass which makes it possible to drive straight through an intersection at full speed. Second is that of the traffic

CENTRAL PARK—1858—USED THE UNDERPASS

circle which makes it possible to turn from one road into another without a stop. It was inevitable that these two ideas should be combined. The result is the "cloverleaf" intersection. The complete cloverleaf pattern provides separate channels for through traffic, right- and left-hand turns. Through traffic keeps straight on over or under the other road. A right turn is made on the diagonal to the right of the driver. To make a left turn, the driver continues on the through traffic lane to the far side of the underpass, turns right, and

[95]

THE CLOVERLEAF—TRANSITIONAL IMPROVEMENT—BUT NOT THE ANSWER

makes a complete circle along the border of one of the four leaves which are ramped, connecting lower and upper road levels.

In comparison with an ordinary intersection, it is manifestly a very superior but expensive structure. When built at the crossing of two heavily traveled highways it may result in a saving of countless vehicle hours a year, as well as innumerable lives. But it is not the final solution. Although there is no light to stop the traffic, the left turn has to be constructed with such a sharp curve that cars must reduce speed to between eight and ten miles an hour to turn left safely. For an individual driver, this loss of speed may represent nothing more than an annoyance. But if traffic in the right-hand lane is heavy, the reduced speed of the car making a left-hand turn is reflected back to the rest of the cars behind, and the old familiar wasteful traffic jam appears again.

If an intersection was crucial to a motorist yesterday, it was not because his car was fast, but because it was not dependable. His brakes were not good; they might make him coast across the road when traffic was against him. His engine might stall as he crossed. The problem today is not the physical fact of difficulty in crossing streams of traffic, but those continual slight pauses of a minute or so—the equivalent of miles of travel. The solution is a continuous flow of traffic with speed and safety.

In place of the present system of prohibitive and directive control, there should be a system that functions automatically. Such a system includes both the highway and the driver. The highway, ideally designed, must be self-functioning; and the driver must function easily as part of it.

Look ahead twenty years to a picture of the crossing point of two major two-directional highway routes. Here seven lanes of traffic move in four directions safely, easily, and with no diminution of speed.

The straight-ahead, free movement of through traffic on all lanes is accomplished by use of the underpass. Both right and left turns are made at fifty-mile speed only, on additional lanes entirely separate from those carrying the through traffic. The motorways incorporate automatically controlled speed reduction points enabling cars to reduce to fifty miles an hour before reaching the intersection approaches. A driver desiring to turn right onto the crossing motorway must be in the right lane of the fifty-mile-an-hour group. The auto-

TRAFFIC FLOW ON PRESENT DAY CLOVERLEAF

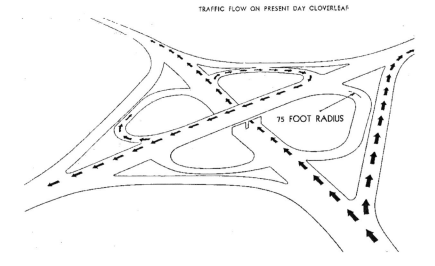

75 FOOT RADIUS

THE CROSSING POINT OF TWO FUTURE MOTORWAYS

Futurama Photo by Richard Garrison

matic motorway control provides for his crossing safely into this lane. At a
point approximately two and a half miles from the intersection his car is eased
to the right out of the through-traffic flow and he travels along a paralleling
lane which becomes a ramped curve to the right. The grade is easy, the gener-
ous curve scarcely perceptible. As this curving lane nears the crossing motorway it straightens out, and the car traveling over it gradually flows into the
outside fifty-mile through-traffic lane. If a driver on the motorway wants to
make a left turn at one of these intersections, he must do so from the left fifty-
mile lane. From this lane he diverges to the left into a separate parallel lane,
speeds along on a gently ramping curve sweeping to the left, parallels the crossing motorway and gradually merges into a space in the flow of cars moving

[98]

in the innermost fifty-mile lane. Speed and spacing on this intersection are controlled automatically and there is no interference with the motorway traffic. The turning-off lanes are elevated or depressed so that there is no interference. This new type of intersection occupies no greater area than the cloverleaf of 1940, when the proportion of the motorway and its capacity of traffic in comparison with present-day roads are taken into consideration.

Although the cost of constructing such an intersection would be considerably more than that of constructing today's cloverleaf, that too costs more than the intersection of former times; and where traffic is heavy there is an increase in safety, speed, comfort, and economy that is as great as that provided by the cloverleaf over previous intersections. The economy in this case is not derived from a reduction in original construction costs, but from a very real, cumulative dollars-and-cents saving to the motorists who use it.

In discussing the problems of traffic on the highways, in the preceding chapter, it was pointed out that physical means built into the highway are possible solutions for overcoming the dangers of traffic and the retardation of

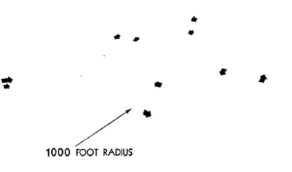

1000 FOOT RADIUS

traffic flow; but that the adaptation of advanced scientific principles to provide a guide operating completely automatically in conjunction with the highway and the car offered the only solution to the traffic problem on a straight stretch of highway. Similar dangerous and inefficient traffic conditions exist in regard to the highway intersection. To alleviate these conditions it is possible to build an advanced type of highway intersection such as that just described.

Suppose for a minute that all cars on a highway operated on a cog track, within the road surface; that they were spaced equal distances apart on all highways, and that they were driven on this cog track at equal speeds. With such a physically controlled system it would be possible at an intersection to control the cars on one highway to make them pass through the spaces between cars on the crossing highway and vice versa, with complete safety and at any speed. This same control can be obtained by adapting the electro-magnetic control utilized for regulating the car speed and spacing along uninterrupted stretches of highway. The application of such automatic control to the intersection would provide for continuous infiltration of the two crossing streams of traffic, both streams of traffic operating continuously at constant speed, without interruption, and without physical separation.

Infiltration is a military term used to denote a method of attack by which the attacking troops sift through the enemy line and are re-formed when the objective is reached. This word "infiltration" aptly describes the operation of an automatic control of intersecting traffic. The method of providing a continuous and uninterrupted flow of through traffic at any intersection is based on the automatic regulation of uniform spacing of cars in their respective lanes and the maintenance of a constant speed in all lanes. Added to this fundamental requirement is the need for control between cars in different lanes and the correlation of the control mechanism of the intersecting highways.

One factor important to this concept and important to all traffic flow is that maneuvering and turning lanes are outside and apart from through lanes. As rural highways approach an intersection they should be widened by one lane on each side to provide for this. In the case of urban streets where such widening is impossible, it is necessary to keep the outside or curb lane free of parked cars and through traffic in order that this lane be always available for maneuvering. Also important is the radius of curves used on intersecting highways. They should be of sufficient magnitude to permit cars turning from one route into the other without reducing speed. Present-day city streets with their small curb radii will not allow this, so that turns must be made at reduced speeds.

With these physical requirements and means of automatic control, any type of intersection or junction at grade can be made safe and efficient. Cars traveling directly through an intersection remain on the straight through lanes of the highway and maintain their speed and direction without change and without interruption. They weave through spaces provided between the cars in the crossing traffic. This process of infiltration or cross-weaving goes on continuously. Uniform car-to-car spacing and speed are maintained in both directions at all times. The parallel maneuvering lanes lead directly into the curves necessary for making a right-hand turn. Here, too, there is no interruption and a car, after taking the curve, automatically flows into the line of through traffic in the new direction which it desires to take. This maneuver is no different from that which would take place on the physically separated type of intersection previously described.

Cars proposing to make a left-hand turn will also draw over into the right-hand maneuvering lane but instead of following the sweeping curve to the right will continue straight ahead. At a designated point in this lane, the car will automatically start a left turn. In making this turn, it will cross the

[101]

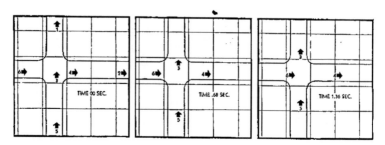

AUTOMATICALLY CONTROLLED SPEED AND SPACING WILL PERMIT MAXIMUM NUMBER OF CARS

through lanes of traffic to reach the maneuvering lane parallel to the lanes of traffic which travel in the new direction which the car is to take. From the maneuvering lane the car will flow into the regular traffic stream. Again, this infiltration process is made possible by the correlation of the control method provided in each lane of traffic.

It becomes necessary to provide accurate predetermined spacing of cars, and to maintain uniform speed in each lane as well as in each of the intersecting highways, and a definite and fixed relation between these factors in each of the lanes of traffic. When that is done, this type of intersection can be applied, regardless of the number of lanes operating in the highway, and regardless of the speed of travel in these lanes.

A free-flowing traffic system necessarily must consider the small with the great; it must solve all the problems that are an everyday occurrence to every driver of a car. The retardation to the smooth flow of traffic on the highways and streets of this country starts way back at the smallest intersection and progressively gets worse as the volume of traffic increases.

In spite of the fact that the problems at the large intersection are more obvious than they are at the small crossroad, the curative measures needed in both situations are similar. They may differ in detail and degree, but they

[102]

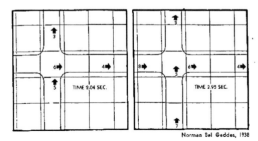

TIME 2.04 SEC.

TIME 2.95 SEC.

Norman Bel Geddes, 1938

TO PASS THROUGH SPACING BETWEEN THEM

should be examined from the same viewpoint. In all intersections, the following standards should be maintained: 1) the radii of the curves should be adapted to the prescribed speed on the intersecting roads so that speed can be maintained without interruption; 2) the view from every direction should extend far enough so that all approaching cars will be plainly visible; 3) curves should be banked to facilitate comfortable maintenance of speed; 4) wherever practicable, a car control system should operate which will provide for the infiltration of traffic without interruption.

Every intersection in the country today is obsolete because the fundamental precepts of traffic flow—safety, comfort, speed and economy—are not considered as a unit but are chosen as separate items on which to base new developments. One intersection considers safety only as its foundation, neglecting the other vital considerations; another is constructed under the rules of comfort. Rarely are both safety and economy of time built into the same traffic crossing. And as long as these fundamentals are allowed to be broken up, just so long will intersections remain obsolete.

FULL SPEED THROUGH BOTTLENECKS

6

WHAT is a bottleneck? It isn't just congestion. Congestion is a general term—something that applies to the forty-eight states, with special application to Greater New York, greater Los Angeles, Detroit and a good many other greater and lesser places. A bottleneck is something specific—a narrowing space causing convergence, like a funnel. A bottleneck is a special phase of the problem of converging traffic. It is the place where a greater number of traffic lanes funnel up to a given point than there are lanes available to take the resulting volume beyond the point. No highway engineer would consciously design a bottleneck. Yet there are so many varieties of the species that they bear classification.

THIS WAS DONE PURPOSELY
Camera Guild

Acme

THIS ISN'T INTENTIONAL

SLOW
ROUGH PAVEMENT
AHEAD

COUNTY LINE EFFICIENCY

One of the most frequent might be called the "county-line bottleneck." This occurs when a fine glittering four-lane highway suddenly stops, like the end of an expression of local pride, at an invisible boundary. The implication seems to be that there is no point in driving farther. It happens because some-one has planned a four-lane road in one county, and the next county joins it with just a two-lane road. It is due to lack of coordinated planning. Beyond the line the road may become a two-lane macadam job, of pre-Prohibition vintage.

Type two is the "detour bottleneck." That occurs when road repair work—widening or reconstruction—blocks either part or all of the roadway. In the first instance, two lanes of traffic have to fight their way through one. In the second, traffic is turned off into the busy wilderness known as a detour. The detour road, it seems, is never as good as the regular road. Even if the detour has adequate width, cars are inevitably slowed down due to one reason or another, which soon affects those far back along the regular road. It is only temporary, but it is a bottleneck just the same.

Type three might be termed the "big building bottleneck." A department store in a crowded section of town prospers. After it has added escalators and sub-basements, it takes on extra stories and a series of annexes. On the morn-ings of special sales, there is a pedestrian queue outside the building all around the block. Twice as many customers are entering the store as did five years ago. In that period the number of trucks backing up to the receiving entrances

[108]

has doubled. Likewise the number of delivery trucks. But during all this growth, no change has been made in the street pattern around the store. The streets retain the same form and capacity as they did five years ago when the store did half as much business.

Type four, by now renowned in song and story, is the "stadium bottleneck." It occurs in short but frequent and very dramatic periods on Saturday afternoons, holidays, and special occasions around such places of pilgrimage as the Yale Bowl, Soldier Field, or the Olympic Stadium in Los Angeles. At three o'clock a hundred thousand people are herding toward a flag-topped amphitheater. At five o'clock they are herding out of it. The stadium has been designed for just such mass movement. It is usually emptied, without fuss or casualty, within fifteen minutes after the final whistle. But the roads around it were not designed for such movement. Los Angeles may say that since the University doesn't pay taxes on its land there is no reason why citizens should spend millions to make the football fans comfortable. In the meantime, the answer to a hundred thousand people is—a hundred traffic cops. This type of bottleneck could have been prevented by good planning when the approaches were built. The traffic problem around the stadium is as much a pedestrian one as a motor car problem. A bottleneck does not merely apply to motor cars. A street in a large city, that passes a public school from which

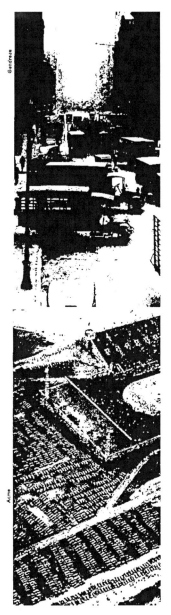

Above: THE CITY STREET BOTTLENECK
Below: PEDESTRIAN PROBLEM SOLVED. TRAFFIC PROBLEM UNSOLVED

thousands of children surge forth twice daily, is a very dangerous bottleneck.

Everyone has his own favorite roadway funnel. Like the fisherman boasting of his catch, he may be inclined to gloat sardonically over the length of the stream of cars trying to get through that particular edge of hell. The high-pressure commuters of Westchester County, New York, have a regional record in the bottleneck at Fleetwood, where the four-lane artery connecting two great new parkways suddenly humps, drops down a steep grade, and corkscrews into a two-lane bridge spanning the New York Central tracks. What makes this contender for the questionable record dramatic is that traffic approaching it comes upon it unexpectedly, after having become accustomed to miles of easy high-speed highway travel. The traffic which had gradually loosened up and spread out is suddenly telescoped, jamming and sputtering on the steep grades to the bridgehead almost in the character of a camel trying to push through the eye of a needle.

There is no use going on classifying. The engineering features of the Holland Tunnel are excellent, as has been previously pointed out; its service during moderate traffic conditions is adequate; but due to its multiple approaches it also is a perfect bottleneck. The cause here was high engineering costs. Removal of natural barriers involved such immense expenditure that it was decided to keep the tunnel down to a two-lane system. But the lanes that approach it do not add up to two. They are so many in number and capacity that at peak hours they develop a volume of traffic that cannot be com-

TWENTY-SEVEN LANES TRYING TO GET INTO TWO LANES   Port of New York Authority

pressed into the tunnel without considerable delay and confusion.

One of the most common forms of bottleneck occurs at bridgeheads and is essentially the same as that created at the tunnel entrance. At the fag end of holidays or week-ends, almost everyone has been exposed time after time, summer after summer, to that most dismal of all motoring experiences: driving back to the city across a bridge. It need not be a drawbridge, where delay can be understood. It may be a big suspension bridge which is inadequate to handle its traffic. While you are still miles away, the car ahead of you and the cars ahead of that, on and on to the unseen bridge, slow down. You drive as close together as freight cars, though not as fast as the slowest freight. It is not driving. Hopelessly often, it is a dead halt. There is no splendor in the sunset. All the fun is drained out of the holiday. You are numbed to any emotion except exasperation.

No one on the road seems to be getting anywhere. Fenders scrape, collars wilt and reaching the bridge becomes not a matter of minutes but of hours. There is no compensating pleasure once you come upon it, long after nightfall. Like every car ahead, you await your turn for this precious road space arched across the water. Other lines of traffic feed slowly in before you have a chance at it. Then, you are on the bridge. Harried drivers are still picking their opportunity to slip into a faster moving lane, despite warning signs to the contrary. Outgoing traffic is cut to a minimum, but still cars from the overcrowded incoming lanes encroach upon it.

Just as the pace of highway development has not kept up with the pace of automobile development, so it is true that bridge development has not kept up with highway development. Most of America's tens of thousands of bridges were built in the era of slower traffic moving on a two-lane road. When the time came, the road was widened. Traffic sped up. But it wasn't such an easy matter to widen a bridge. Perhaps the bridge should have been replaced entirely. Maybe the Highway Commission couldn't afford such an item that year. The road was built, but the bridge was postponed. The result is that the high-speed traffic which has been flowing for miles along the highway suddenly has to slow down at the bridgehead with the inevitable jam of cars approaching the bridge.

The State of Indiana, for example, has not ignored the work of highway improvement. In the past few years it has widened 1800 miles of state highway—the major roads to 100 feet and the secondary roads to 80 feet. But the Chairman of its State Highway Commission complains that nearly 2000 bridges and culverts along the system are so narrow that they alone cause great delay and many deaths each year. To replace them by adequate structures, he says, would cost about 25 billion dollars.

Just how the lag operates is shown by the story of the Queensboro Bridge, opened in 1909 to carry a fast-growing volume of traffic between midtown Manhattan and developments on Long Island. At first it had three lanes; then two more were added. In 1931 an upper deck was opened, giving the bridge a total of seven lanes. This sounded like continual improvement. But at the same time there were repeated efforts to open up and spread out the bridge's approach plazas. While city officials were struggling with approach property and while the bridge was taking on a lane here and there, the lanes feeding the bridge were increasing at a much greater rate. Today there are, estimated conservatively, six streets or twenty-four lanes on each side of the river. Easily more than fifty lanes of traffic feed into this bridge from both ends. The bridge has only seven lanes to cope with the situation. This is the situation today, and settlements are still rising by the hundreds on Long Island. The approach land, not bought in time, is now prohibitive in cost. The Queensboro Bridge will never be able to cope with this problem.

Famous spans like this or the Eads Bridge at St. Louis were built to meet the conditions and requirements that prevailed at the time they were designed. Their designs did not anticipate the automotive era. Conditions have changed entirely. The old roadways which were built to meet those conditions have perhaps been replaced, but the bridges linger on because financially they obsolesce far more slowly than any other highway structure. It takes sixty to eighty years to amortize a bridge. The obvious conclusion is that bridges designed today should not be planned just for today's needs. They should take into consideration all the possible needs that may arise during their lifetime

Underwood & Underwood   QUEENSBORO BRIDGE, NEW YORK

—a life that is likely to exceed the classically allotted three-score and ten.

The Bay Bridge at San Francisco consists of two decks, with six lanes for high-speed automobile traffic on the top deck, and three lanes for bus and truck traffic on the lower deck, which is also designed to carry an electric railway line. But perhaps the key fact about the bridge is not the bridge itself but what happens before one gets to it. There are four and a half miles of approaches. They include ramps leading on and off, overpasses and underpasses to avoid intersecting traffic, and on the Oakland side a distribution system which goes beyond the modern cloverleaf pattern. The intention of the design-

BAY BRIDGE, SAN FRANCISCO

ers was to get an immense volume of traffic across the bridge quickly, without slowing down. In the first full year of operation, 9,109,349 vehicles made the crossing. Planning had worked.

The Bay Bridge is not especially broad, as great spans go. There is a lesson in that. When one sees a congested bridge, one is likely to think the trouble is that it is too narrow; the real trouble is that it does not have enough lanes. The earliest covered bridges suggested the possibility of increasing the height of a bridge rather than its width. A two-decker bridge is a rarity in our midst. But there is no reason why we should be limited even to two decks.

Bottlenecks within our highway system can only be eliminated or avoided by a comprehensive and long-range planning program. County-line bottlenecks would not occur if there were cooperative highway planning between adjoining counties. Detour bottlenecks would not exist if highway construction undertakings were adequately planned before construction started, so as to provide adequate detour routes for the existing traffic on the highway under construction or under repair. Big building bottlenecks would not exist if there were adequate town and city planning programs, incorporating and making allowance for growth of the city and town, as well as increased traffic resulting from such growth. Stadium bottlenecks exist only because highway approaches were not planned in conjunction with the planning of the stadium, or the selection of the location for the stadium was not made with regard to the traffic facilities available.

Bridges and tunnels across natural barriers to highway traffic are the most common type of bottleneck, and therefore the most flagrant example of lack of planning. Bridges built before the full magnitude of automobile traffic was foreseen become bottlenecks on the highway leading to the bridge when this highway is widened to carry a greater volume of traffic without, at the same time, widening or increasing the capacity of the bridge. Bridges and tunnels

[115]

built since the automobile era have also, in many instances, been constructed without development of their approaches and the highways leading to them.

Bridges for automobile traffic should be built to provide for expansion of the bridge itself—that is, to provide for the construction of a greater number of lanes as traffic density increases. At the same time they should provide, in their plaza approaches and on the highways leading to them, facilities for handling expansion of the approaching highways and the bridge-approach plaza.

APPROACH TO NEW YORK'S GEORGE WASHINGTON BRIDGE

Fairchild

[116]

Here is a glimpse into the future twenty years from now, at a suspension bridge that carries a motorway across a wide river. The approach plaza where bridge traffic is collected and distributed reaches far from the bridge. There is no bridgehead congestion. The motorway is two-directional as it enters the approach plaza. Its design shows four fifty-mile lanes with separators; a grass strip; two seventy-five-mile lanes with separators; a grass strip; and a hundred-mile lane. On this motorway, cars are traveling toward the bridge.

On a similar seven-lane road, and separated from this one by a grass strip, are cars traveling in the opposite direction. As this double motorway approaches a town feeder boulevard running at right angles to it, the hundred-and seventy-five-mile lanes start on a rising grade with the roadway carried on columns. The fifty-mile lanes are gradually drawn in to take a position under the high-speed lanes forming a two-tier viaduct that overpasses the feeder boulevard. The town feeder has eight lanes of fifty-mile traffic moving in opposite directions. As the traffic nears the motorway, the two outside lanes make a right turn on a radius that will allow a fifty-mile undiminished speed, ramp up and enter below the two-tier structure to form a third tier. At the same point a re-

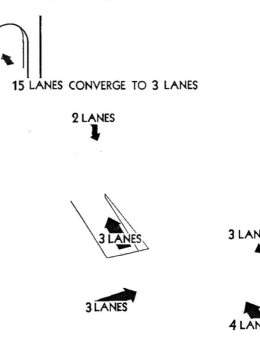

15 LANES CONVERGE TO 3 LANES

2 LANES

3 LANES

3 LANES

3 LANES

4 LANES

GEORGE WASHINGTON BRIDGE APPROACH PROBLEM

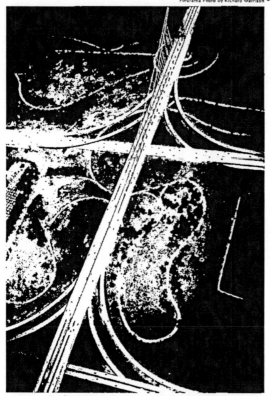

Futurama Photo by Richard Garrison

FUTURE BRIDGE PLAZA WILL ELIMINATE BOTTLENECK APPROACHES

verse procedure occurs and cars come from the bridge on two lanes turning left and ramping down to form a two-lane strip along the town feeder. On the opposite side of the motorway, similar provisions are made for traffic approaching from that direction.

The approach structure takes shape as a three-tier viaduct; eight fifty-mile lanes on the lower level, eight fifty-mile lanes on the middle level, and four seventy-five-mile and two hundred-mile lanes on the top level. It continues ramping up; now it crosses a second town feeder boulevard. More cars are gathered in by the same system as before. Still the structure rises: now it consists of four tiers. All the time each lane preserves its own integrity. No one cuts in. No one fears collision. No one slows down. Traffic moves without delay.

This bridge with its huge stainless steel towers is designed to allow for expansion. The towers are not double piers. They are single masts. Four tiers of highway run one above the other, keeping the bridge relatively narrow. The need for cross-bracing is reduced. Half of the traffic lanes hang outside the great spires on cantilevered supports. Only those lanes necessary immediately need be built at first, then as more are required they are added. The original structure is designed to accommodate itself to such expansion. The lanes head across the span. It is not obvious to the driver when he leaves it, for the distributing plaza at the other end merely continues the shape and speed of the lanes. The bridge is not a special structure that interrupts the motorway. It has not been tinkered with or lamely widened to meet the toll of traffic. It has been built along the lines of one unified and eloquent principle: to provide full road width and full road speed at every point along the highway.

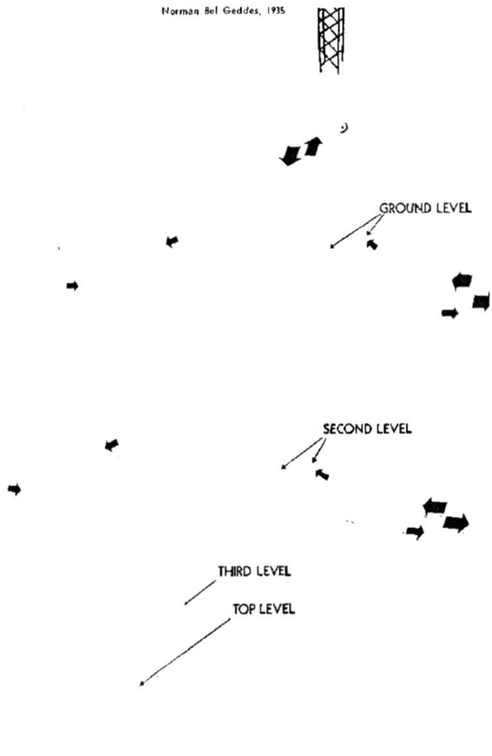

No bottleneck is ever created intentionally. In fact, the cause for the bottle-

Norman Bel Geddes, 1935

GROUND LEVEL

SECOND LEVEL

THIRD LEVEL

TOP LEVEL

TRAFFIC FLOW ON APPROACHES TO FUTURE MULTI-DECK BRIDGE

BRIDGES WILL CARRY SAME NUMBER OF LANES AS APPROACHES

neck is probably the only cause in the world which can find no defenders. Therefore, it is not enough simply to point out that bottlenecks should not exist; it is not enough to point an accusing finger at a flagrant example and say that it is a flagrant example. Once a road is built, the points along it where congestion occur are only too obvious. The trick is to ascertain these points in advance, to prevent them. Therefore, any road, before it is built, should be

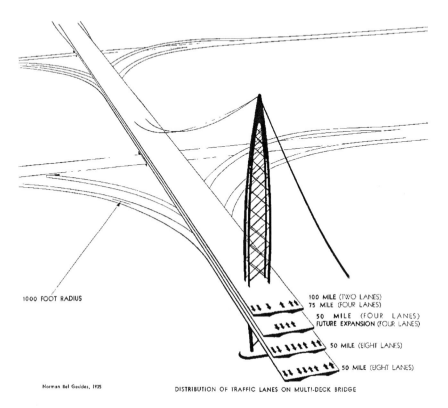

1000 FOOT RADIUS

100 MILE (TWO LANES)
75 MILE (FOUR LANES)
50 MILE (FOUR LANES)
FUTURE EXPANSION (FOUR LANES)
50 MILE (EIGHT LANES)
50 MILE (EIGHT LANES)

Norman Bel Geddes, 1935   DISTRIBUTION OF TRAFFIC LANES ON MULTI-DECK BRIDGE

analyzed in regard to all its possible future uses. The highway designer must determine what kinds of traffic will be using the road, at what point on the road the greatest number of cars will get on it, and where most of the cars will want to get off. It is possible to determine this by thorough traffic surveys and by population analysis. Elimination of bottlenecks can be achieved through intelligent, far-sighted planning in advance of road construction.

DAYLIGHT STANDARDS FOR NIGHT DRIVING

WHEN a man ventured forth at night through the streets of eighteenth century London or New York, he carried a lantern to light the way between puddles and pitfalls. If he was a member of the "gentry" he hired a boy to carry the lantern for him. When, in the following century, a coal miner reached the bottom of the shaft and began his way through dark wet tunnels, he lit the light fixed to his helmet. Both Victorian miner and Georgian city-reveller found the lantern perfectly suited to their purpose; as they groped and twisted, the light twisted with them.

In 1940 people are still groping around with lanterns. The only difference is that now they are hung on the front of a car or truck, and the rate of groping through the darkness is between thirty and sixty miles an hour. Of course, this lantern is a good deal brighter than its ancestors—so bright, in fact, that it succeeds in blinding anyone driving toward it. It blinds him so effectively that after its flash has passed, it takes his eye almost a minute to readjust itself to darkness, during which time, still half-blind, he may be traveling as much as half a mile. It is a most diabolically effective instrument.

A CAT BEGINS TO LIVE AT NIGHT Underwood & Underwood

To a greater or lesser degree everyone is blind at night. Too much light is as bad as too little. Headlights are not bright enough to light the road ahead but too bright for the approaching driver. The shift from darkness to brilliance and back again is too swift. Twenty years ago, visibility distance with automobile headlights on light-colored dry roads was from 200 to 250 feet. On dark or wet roads, the visibility was virtually nil. Today, while great advances have been made in the construction of cars, and great increases in their speed, the visibility of headlights has not greatly changed. Driving at a speed of more than 40 miles an hour on an unlighted highway, even though the road be dry, the night clear and the high-beam headlights burning brightly, the driver might just as well be blindfolded so far as his visibility is related to the speed of his car. Add to this the fact that when the car is rounding a curve, its headlights point diagonally off, missing the roadside entirely and sometimes reducing the visibility to 50 feet, increasing the driver's blindness still more.

If automobile headlights comply with all legal requirements, they will enable a driver to pick out a dark object on an unlighted road only about 150 feet ahead of him. The Police Department of Pasadena, California, became very much interested in this fact. Their research taught them that a car driving at 60 miles an hour could under no circumstances be stopped in less than 200 feet. This established the possibility that if a pedestrian was crossing the path of a car moving at 60 miles an hour and if he was 150 feet ahead of it, he would be dragged 50 feet before the car came to a stop. This would happen even if the driver applied his brakes the instant he saw him, and even if his brakes were working perfectly.

In general, public authorities studying the problem of night accidents have paid relatively scant attention to the darkness factor. They have accepted the increase in traffic fatalities as being the result of more cars and greater speed. This seems a logical assumption until one breaks down the totals of fatalities into daylight accidents and night accidents. Then one finds an astonishing fact. In 1937 automobile accidents caused more deaths than fires, typhoid, diphtheria, railroads, airplanes,

BUT 21,900 AUTOISTS DIED AT NIGHT IN A YEAR

and ships all put together. They numbered 39,700. Of this total, 23,800 people were killed at night. This would be understandable if by far the greater volume of traffic moved at night. But as everyone knows, it doesn't. Only about one-third of all motor traffic moves at night. And yet two-thirds of all fatal motor accidents occur at night.

Accident figures emphasize that not only are there more accidents by night than by day, but that the severity of night-time accidents is far greater than that of daytime accidents. One in every forty-nine daytime motor vehicle injuries proves fatal. But at night there is one death for every twenty-six injuries. Furthermore, this discrepancy gets greater every year. In the period from 1930 to 1937 inclusive, there was a 2 per cent decline in daytime accident deaths, while there was an *increase* of almost 30 per cent in night-

THE LIGHT THAT FAILED

Gendreau

time fatalities. These figures point to an obvious conclusion. Whereas efforts have been made and are being made to improve conditions of daytime driving, little has been done to overcome the greater hazards of the road at night.

It is significant, too, that the greatest number of fatalities occurs between the hours of 5 P.M. and 8 P.M. During these hours in winter, when the night falls quickly, more than twice as many deaths occur as in summer when the light lingers. This is in spite of the fact that the traffic volume during this hour in summer is apt to be greater than it is during the same hour in winter. Darkness itself, then, must be the hazard-creating element. It is true that at night there are a greater number of fatigued, intoxicated or irresponsible drivers. It is also true that there is a heavier component of large commercial vehicles in the traffic stream. But the main fact is that night creates an entirely different kind of traffic. A new relationship is established between driver and highway. When the sun goes down there is no change in the car or the road, or, necessarily, the driver or the weather. But there is the change from light to darkness, all-important because it makes the driver orient himself to an entirely new set of conditions.

For instance, it has been established that for a driver traveling at 50 miles an hour, safety requires that he have unobstructed vision for at least 575 feet ahead. Yet when that driver is placed upon that road at night, without lights along the way and only his own headlights to go by, his maximum visibility is about 200 feet, and a set of headlights coming down the highway from the opposite direction—even if they are very low in intensity—reduces the driver's perception, already dangerously limited, by 60 per cent.

Obviously what is lacking is proper lighting. The remedy usually offered is to illuminate the highways themselves, so that drivers will not have to depend on automobile headlights. But even highway lighting is not necessarily proper lighting. If it is incorrect in design or inadequate in strength—and this is the case on most highways which have been lighted so far—it creates still another danger factor.

A lighted street is safer than an unlighted one. But during what period should a highway be lit? In the British Empire there is a law that specifies a moment called "lighting-up time" which varies from day to day in accordance with the sun's disappearance. A small English town, apparently eager to augment this ruling, hung upon its lampposts a curfew regulation which ended with the following ironic definition of darkness: "It is dark when the street lights are on."

Except near the equator where night comes suddenly, there is a considerable interval between sundown and night. Darkness comes gradually. One's eyes become adjusted to the increasing dimness of vision. Only after the street lights are on does one look up with a dazzled start and realize that darkness is coming in earnest. This dazzlement does not come from any notable contrast between twilight and the daylight that preceded it. The realization that it is dark comes from the contrast between the bright spot of the lamplight itself and the comparative darkness around it.

[129]

The type of lamp and standard used on those highways which are actually lighted today has been copied from the types traditionally used on city streets. But just as the light on the "great white ways" of American cities is no longer white, but a confusion of flickering commercial signs of every known hue, so the hopeful attempt to illuminate highways with lofty standards has become rather tangled up in the maze of roadside floodlights, neon lights, lunch-wagon lights, traffic lights, and flashing headlights. How haphazard the thinking behind conventional highway illumination is, is suggested by the way many highway lighting systems are administered. Until midnight or 1 A.M. there is fairly adequate illumination. Then, suddenly, the whole system is switched off. Traffic has not stopped. No curfew has rung. There are plenty of people who have to go on driving for the rest of the night—the doctor on an emergency call, the through tourist, the long-distance truckman, the late home-comer—but they get no help. The reason given for the shutdown is, of course, economy. But that doesn't make it any easier or safer for the man who happens to be on the road at 1:05 A.M rather than 12:55 A.M.

ROAD SIGNS FOR CATS   Gendreau

5←ARDSLEY
7←DOBBS FERRY
8←HASTINGS
12←YONKERS
N. Y. STATE HIGHWAY

A great deal of experimenting is being done on new types of lamps for highway lighting. Most important of these are the sodium vapor lamps and the mercury vapor lamps. And although these lamps have not yet reached perfection, they are from an engineering standpoint a step in the right direction and have much to recommend them. They are both more penetrating and more economical than regular lights. One of their drawbacks, how-

SODIUM SAFETY LIGHTS

ever, is that the eerie pallor which they give to the highway scene is decidedly unpleasant to the motorist. Rapid progress is also being made in improving the efficiency of the incandescent filament type of lamp. New incandescent lamps of high intensity, supplemented by improved reflectors lining the luminaire, are already in use, a notable example of which is found on New Jersey's White Horse Pike. Sodium vapor and mercury vapor have also been combined with incandescent lamps to form a new fluorescent type of light. As compared with regular incandescent lamps, the sodium vapor lamps give nearly three times as much light for the amount of electricity used. In New Jersey, accidents have been cut in half where sodium light has been employed. This type of lighting was first used in 1933, and is especially effective for wide streets because it distributes its light broadly.

In addition to direct lighting methods, there are in use today several types of indirect lighting systems, consisting of large reflector buttons which do not have a light source of their own but which reflect back upon the highway the light from approaching headlamps. They outline the road for a mile ahead except at curves or where they are obstructed. Their great virtue

CURVES LIT BY INCANDESCENT LUMINAIRES

lies in the fact that they define a roadway at no cost whatever other than that of installation. They are not intended to replace highway lights, but simply to supplement them. The most recently developed reflector buttons are approximately eight times more powerful than any previously used.

Not only are experiments being made with different types of lighting, but also with the manner of their installation. The lighting system installed on the upper deck of a double-decked viaduct in Cincinnati consists of lighting units placed in the balustrade of the viaduct which throw their light horizontally across the road surface from both sides, rather than down on the surface from high above.

Lack of uniformity among state laws on intensity of headlights, their location and their general characteristics makes progress in the correction of the problem difficult. Obviously there can be no great advancement in practical lighting until the authorities get together and agree. It may be found necessary to set up a central body, such as the Bureau of Standards, to arrive at a unified control of this universal problem. Under today's system of local responsibility for lighting, there is apt to be needless duplication of research and study by people inadequately equipped for such a large task. A centralizing agency could collect and coordinate the scattered research on the subject, test new methods, and recommend modern types of lighting after sufficiently broad experimentation had proved their merit.

Scientific experimentation has recently resulted in the perfection of a new material for use in automobile headlight lenses and in automobile windshields which promises great improvement in efficient highway illumination by headlights without corresponding headlight glare. This material, called Polaroid, was developed by Edwin H. Land, in 1934. It is a flexible, transparent film that in appearance somewhat resembles cellophane. This material acts to comb out or regiment the light which passes through it, so that the light which has

SAFETY RIBS BY DAY AND REFLECTED ILLUMINATION BY NIGHT

FINDING A THREE-LEAF CLOVER BY NIGHT

been transmitted through it vibrates in only one plane, whereas normally light vibrates in all planes. This type of light is called polarized light, and has been known to science for over 200 years. However, this property of light could not be made use of commercially until the introduction of Polaroid, because of the excessive cost of materials existing for the purpose of polarizing light. The great advantage of Polaroid is in the fact that it can be produced practically and economically on a commercial scale.

In a beam of light such as that from a normal automobile headlight waves are vibrating in every plane along the beam. However, replace the headlight lens with a sheet of polarized material, and its crystals will comb out all of the vibrations except those vibrating in a particular plane. The beam of light which has passed through the polarized material will then have light vibrations in only one plane. Then take a second sheet of the polarized material and place it in the path of light that has passed through the first. If its crystals are parallel to those of the first sheet, the light will get through. If they are at right angles, the light will be stopped.

This characteristic of polarized light is made use of in the automobile in the following way: a piece of polarized material is sandwiched between layers of glass from the headlight lens of the automobile. This is so placed that the light passing through it is vibrating in a plane at 45 degrees to the road. Then a similar piece is made a part of the windshield of the car, and oriented in such a way that when two cars approach each other along a highway the plane of the polarized light from the headlights of one car is at right angles to the polarized plane provided by the windshield of the opposing car. Therefore the rays of light from the opposing car cannot pass through the windshield of the approaching car, and the headlights, instead of glaring at the driver, appear as a very faint glow indicating merely the position of the oncoming automobile. At the same time, all of the light from both cars which is still on the road surface clearly illuminates the surface and makes it visible as if no other car were approaching. The headlights themselves appear only as faint disks, dim but clearly discernible. With this abolition of glare comes freedom from the usual partial blindness that occurs while two cars are passing.

Of course there is no point in installing polarized material in one car unless it is installed in other cars as well. The effectiveness of this material depends entirely on the passage of a national law. It cannot be applied locally.

A special aspect of the science of lighting is the study of color. First there is the color of the road surface. Everyone who drives at night has experienced the sense of relief that occurs on changing from a black macadam road surface to light gray concrete. The difference is that the concrete has far higher light-reflecting power. Its light background causes objects to stand out in bold relief for a longer distance ahead. Then there is the color of the illumination. Experimental tests are now being conducted with lights that have a green tint. White light, because of its tendency to produce glare, is by no means ideal for the human eye.

These studies and experiments for improved highway lighting, improved headlight illumination and improved road and light colors all tend to relieve the highway illumination problem. But the basic problem is much greater than any of these aspects of it would indicate. The solution can only be obtained by a broad outlook at the whole problem of highway lighting.

On most present-day highways there is either a total absence of light or the kind of lighting that belongs to pre-motor days. The tall handsome lamp-posts that are still set up along the highways seem like sentimental relics of those days. They look a good deal like old-fashioned domestic bridge lamps. It is not necessary that a bridge lamp light up a whole room. It must simply give strong illumination over the book or game on which eyes are focused. The current highway bridge lamp does the same thing. It gives brilliant patches

SODIUM LAMPS REDUCING ALTERNATE SHADED AREAS

of light which alternate with dark areas. Its patches, true enough, are very brilliant. They have to be. If you hang your light way up, you have to make it intense. But the consequence is simple and eloquent: it is glare again.

It is a commonplace, but it bears repeating: everyone is agreed that the best lighting is daylight. That has a corollary. In daylight the vertical objects on the road are dark compared with the light surface of the road. Thus, in order to get the best conditions on the road at night as well, the objects should be left dark, and the horizontal surface lit up.

The problem of keeping a highway continuously illuminated after nightfall is one of cost. But the cost of lighting highways is a comparatively small fraction of their expense. And the results of lighting are greater use of existing roadways, increased speed of night driving and substantial savings in life and property.

In the next twenty years, immense progress is going to be made to eliminate the old hazard of night driving. Cars will still have headlights, of course, to be used on minor roads, but these will probably utilize the advantages of polarized light. Motorways will be lit. But their illumination will be entirely re-studied, not only regarding the equipment itself, but regarding the location of the equipment. Lights will be brought down out of their bridge-lamp elevation and placed closer to the highway surface where their lights may be more effectively used, illuminating the road itself rather than the upper ether. Lights will be so located that they do not shine into the eyes of drivers.

Consider briefly what might prove to be the ideally lit motorway of the future. A long banner of illumination lies ahead. You don't see the continuous strip of tubular lights which has been set along the lanes below the driver's eye level. There is no glare. An even distribution of light covers the road surface. All the headlights of cars are out. Your eyes are never assaulted. Even the color of the light has been selected to relieve eyestrain. There is no more huddling together toward the center of the road. Drivers do no more blinking and groping.

And, late at night, when traffic flow is diminished, the highway still isn't

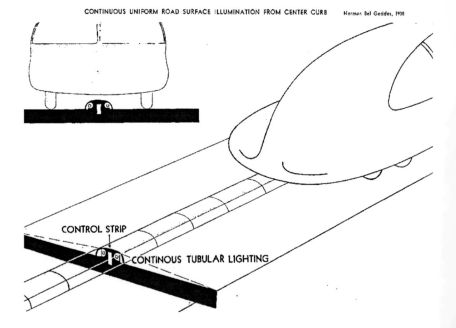

CONTINUOUS UNIFORM ROAD SURFACE ILLUMINATION FROM CENTER CURB   Norman Bel Geddes, 1938

CONTROL STRIP

CONTINOUS TUBULAR LIGHTING

dark and treacherous. Although the system of lights goes off, it doesn't go off according to an arbitrary time schedule, but only for as long as the roadway is unused. The approach of a car causes an automatic device to turn on the lights ahead for a prescribed distance. Lights continuously turn on before each car. Behind the car, the lights turn off until another car approaches. No meters in the powerhouse are ticking off the cost of their operation when lights are not needed. When the motorway is filled to capacity, it is illuminated over its entire length. But when there is a smaller amount of traffic flow, if the space between the cars is greater than the standard distance, there is a dark unilluminated space behind each car.

Over and beyond its efficiency, the system also provides advantages that are likely to be overlooked by pleasure drivers. These advantages result in increased efficiency of night trucking, the economic importance of which is growing every year. Night trucking has to operate under many difficulties. That a nationwide highway lighting system would not only expedite this traffic but also considerably increase it, is not to be doubted. Thus on the new motorway there is full use and at the same time there is economy. There is no wasting of electricity. Also there is not the wasting of time and road investment that comes from inadequately lighted highways. There is not the wasting of property. There is not the wasting of human life.

The time will come when night driving will be regarded as actually more pleasant than driving in the daytime. For the light of the sun is variable and capricious. No one can control its direction or its intensity. But at night the automatic devices of the road will supply an ideal control of light. After all, it is not a revolutionary dream to take lights down off the poles. There is no special witchcraft in the idea of driving along a highway through a self-induced flood of light. These things can be done. There is no reason for drivers to go on being slaves at night when they could so easily be masters.

[139]

FROM THE ATLANTIC TO THE PACIFIC IN ONE DAY

THE first transcontinental trips by automobile brought no great improvement in running time. In 1903, Sewell K. Croker left San Francisco in a two-cylinder Winton and after two months and two days he arrived in New York. The drivers who followed his pioneering example also took about two months.

As long-distance travel by car developed, it was seen that adequate motor roads were a necessity. A better-roads movement, which later developed into the Lincoln Highway Association, was founded in 1912 by Carl G. Fisher, maker of the Prest-O-Lite system of headlights. In order to dramatize this need, Mr. Fisher joined an automobile tour to the Pacific Coast, using a jumble of unmarked roads. The party's cars had to be shoveled out along the way and coaxed over the steep grades. Mr. Fisher described one of the culminating experiences which convinced him of the need for adequate roads as follows: "One night, overtaken by darkness and a drenching rain, I lost my way some nine miles from Indianapolis. At a fork in the road, my car's headlights revealed the base of a road sign, but the sign itself was too high to read. I shinnied up the sign pole, struck a match and read the sign. It directed me to 'Chew

Battle-Ax Plug!' " Armed with this useful information, he continued his trip.

In the specifications for a model section of road drawn up by the Lincoln Highway Association in 1920 many sound principles were formulated. Two of them bear rather directly on Mr. Fisher's agile ascent of the chewing-tobacco sign pole. They are: 1. "The section should be lighted." 2. "Advertising signs should be prohibited along the right of way." Seven years later, the Lincoln Highway between New York and San Francisco was completed and, for the first time, motor cars could travel across the continent on one highway.

The Lincoln Highway falls lamentably short of the needs of motor transport today. The standard right of way advocated in its specifications is 110 feet wide. Over one half of its length, it is only a two-lane road. With the exception of a strip in Nebraska, the road is entirely paved, but most of the paved section is macadam rather than concrete. It is not really a continuous highway but a composite of many highways pieced together. These pieces include spurs, old junctions, a cross-patch of trails and communicating roads, and they pass through 110 cities and 200 towns during their 3056 miles. The Highway was designed to be used by cars operating at a speed of 35 miles an hour and by trucks at 10 miles an hour. Few long-distance drivers today care to drive that slowly.

The failure of the Lincoln Highway is due to lack of vision that did not allow for any substantial improvement in the motor car. It was not primarily, however, a lack of vision on the part of the people who got the Highway built; it was a lack of vision on the part of the people who opposed it. To get the road through at all was a very difficult problem.

To operate profitably on long-distance hauling, truck drivers must maintain 40 or more miles an hour. It is not surprising that they find inadequate for their needs a road designed for average truck speed of 10 miles an hour, and interrupted at intervals of every half mile or so by crossroads. What could show the high mortality of highways more clearly than the fact that a road only twelve years old is already a relic of the era when trucks were required to creep along at 10 miles an hour?

Besides the Lincoln Highway, three other main transcontinental routes exist, the Sante Fe Trail which parallels in part the old wagon road through the Raton Pass in New Mexico, the Broadway of America which is a scenic route from New York passing through Washington, D.C., to San Diego, and the Yellowstone Route which runs from Chicago to the National Park in Wyoming. The shortest distance from coast to coast is 2935 miles from New York to Los Angeles by the Sante Fe and Will Rogers Highways.

In addition to these major transcontinental roads, there are a great many other motor roads which the transcontinental traveler can use. There are one hundred and seventeen numbered routes running east and west for varying distances, and one hundred and seven numbered routes between the nation's northern and southern boundaries. The nomenclature adopted for national highways gives odd numbers to routes running north and south, such as U.S. Highway Number One along the Atlantic seaboard. Even-numbered routes run east and west, as U.S. Highway Number Two, from Eastern Maine to Glacier Park in Northwest Montana. From Rouses' Point, New York, to Sault Ste. Marie on the northern peninsula of Michigan there is a gap in this U.S. Highway, for the shortest distance between these two points lies over Canadian roads.

An official road guide book of 1915 grew lyrical in its attempts to lure motorists westward to the San Francisco World's Fair over the macadamized turnpikes of the East, the fair-weather roads of the Middle West and the natural gravel of Wyoming. The hazards of travel near Fish Springs, Utah, certainly did not frighten the writer of the guide book: "If trouble is experienced, build a sagebrush fire. Mr. Thomas will come with a team. He can see you 20 miles off." John Thomas was an honest man. He had a fixed price. It did not matter whether one or four cars were stuck in the mud; he would haul all of them out for the same price—ten dollars. Mr. Thomas, however, abhorred arguments, and he always had the last word. If the captive motorists ventured to dispute the fee, Mr. Thomas merely raised it to twenty or twenty-five dollars. These were roads which, as Mr. Crocker had demonstrated twelve years before, could be traversed by automobile. But they were certainly not roads designed to facilitate motor travel.

Even today, in cars that can go 70 miles an hour, many motorists take ten days to cross the continent. It is not a question of straight transcontinental travel only. The same conditions exist on north-south routes, or on any long inter-city routes. The 1940 motor car is capable of carrying goods or passengers at sustained speeds on extremely long trips. Yet only a very small percentage of trucks or passenger cars in the United States is driven on long trips. Drivers are not deterred by lack of faith in their cars. But it costs too much—in time, money and energy—to do a long-distance automobile run in the country today. Undoubtedly you or friends of yours have made the trip from coast to coast by car. You will have noticed that the highways along which you drive are by no means the undeviating ways indicated by the delicate lines on the nation's road maps. They are merely connecting links from one town to another which, if followed with sufficient diligence and reference

OFF TO THE WORLD'S FAIR—1915 Brown Bros.

to road maps, bring you eventually to the coast. Even with two or more drivers relieving each other to keep the car moving night and day, it is not possible to make the trip by car as quickly as by train. Average time for the trip by motor is longer than by rail chiefly because the highways used also serve local traffic, which has a very different pace and purpose from that of the cross-country driver.

From an inquisitive tourist's point of view, there may be possible advantages in zigzagging one's way from coast to coast, and coming in contact with a maximum number of one's fellow citizens en route. However, few cross-country drivers who have made the trip, either for business or pleasure, express this sentiment. Travel by road, especially in the case of merchandise, ought to have many superiorities over any other kind of travel. The car and the truck are both capable of sustained high speeds. The pleasure car is under the driver's individual control, thus eliminating the irksome necessity of conforming to prearranged schedules and routes. And as for merchandise, one pound of truck will haul two pounds of freight, while in order to haul the same two pounds of freight on the railroad, it takes eight pounds of freight car.

Engineers could readily design trucks, buses and passenger cars to operate at 100 miles an hour, if proper roads were available for their use. At such speed, the trip from Chicago to San Francisco could be made in about eighteen hours. If new routes are to be planned

Margaret Bourke-White   TRUCKING—OR MONKEY BUSINESS

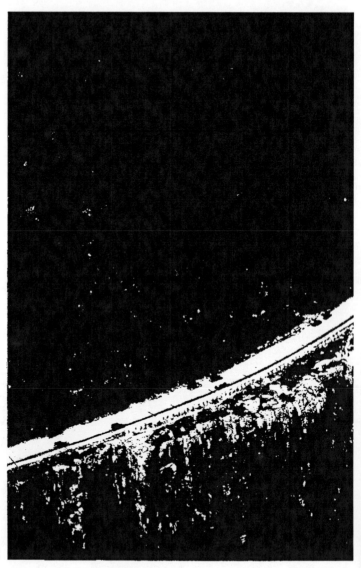

SKIMMING
THE TIP OF
THE PALISADES

today, they should not become obsolete in another twenty years. Therefore designers should think in terms of highways that can be safely used even at 100 miles an hour. Such highways are possible. From the motorist's point of view, the idea of driving at such speed, even with safety, is not yet especially popular, but to no one today does it seem as fantastic, immoral or suicidal as driving at 50 miles an hour seemed to buggy drivers two generations ago. In those days, trains ran through the countryside as fast as the average motor car does today. Now airplanes carrying passengers at 200 miles an hour are commonplace. And yet the same argument persists that was advanced by the driver who whipped up old Dobbin saying, "Anyone who drives faster than I do is driving too fast. A body can't stand it."

It is just as short-sighted for people today to say that cars should not drive at 100 miles an hour as it was of George Washington's physician to warn him that anyone driving over 15 miles an hour would inevitably die of heart-failure. Incidentally, George Washington was never in danger on this account. Average stagecoach speed on his travels was 4 miles an hour.

The sensation of speed is relative. No family now driving in a closed car, on a smooth straight road at 50 miles an hour, experiences the sensation of wind-blown, dust-raising dare-deviltry which made the family group in a 1910 open-model Buick hold on for their lives, as the car achieved a nerve- and spine-racking burst of speed at 12 miles an hour over a rutted roadway.

In 1848, the railroad revolutionized man's concept of speed. A train burning pine knots ran from Boston to Lawrence, Massachusetts, in twenty-six minutes, at the hitherto unheard-of speed of a mile a minute. This was not an ordinary passenger run but a demonstration. The daring newspaper reporters who made the trip "commended themselves to God, and were lying down on the floor where the chance of survival seemed better." It took a week to repair the tracks after this venture, but the concept of a "mile a minute" immediately became firmly established in the popular imagination as top speed. This popular concept became an incentive to faster travel. Today it is as antiquated a measure for top speed as was the 10-mile-an-hour pace at which the first automobile race was run.

Early in 1939, H. Lloyd Child, test pilot, exceeded all known speed records in a dive of more than 575 miles an hour, starting at an altitude of 22,000 feet. No one proposes to drive an automobile that fast, though John Cobb has driven a racing car at 368 miles an hour, which is faster than a shell shot from a mortar. In an airplane, speed is a safety

SPEED IS RELATIVE—SEA BISCUIT BEATS WAR ADMIRA

factor: it is speed which increases the airplane's ability to sustain itself. On today's highways, because of the ever-present chance of coming into contact with another vehicle or a stationary object, speed translates itself into a danger factor. But in 1960, 100 miles an hour will seem no faster than the motor speeds which we now take for granted.

To convert all American roads into high-speed superhighways would be both impracticable and undesirable. But a certain number of motorways where safe, fast driving and an uninterrupted trip would be possible are nevertheless an immediate need. By stimulating the use of motor vehicles, such new motorways would amply pay the cost of construction and would serve as models for the future. For centuries we were content with springless wagons. Is that a reason why we should continue to put up with slow roads?

Imagine a man who wants to drive from the Atlantic Coast to California, not on pleasure bent nor on one of the fancier varieties of business, but in dead earnest on a plain job. Say he drives a truck. He has some highly perishable freight to transport. It has to get across the country quickly. It's nothing more nor less than twelve barrels of oysters that have been hauled out of Chesapeake Bay the day the season opened. The jobber in California can't wait for rail transport. He can't pay for air transport. So he is dependent on high-speed trucking.

At 5:15 in the afternoon, with the trailer loaded, the truckman and his relief driver climb aboard. From the oyster pier the route lies over the improved secondary highways which serve as feeders to the motorway. Twenty-five miles outside Washington they pick up the motorway feeder lanes, built as a unit with the motorway and having the same construction and design characteristics. As the truck bears to the right from the secondary highway at the feeder point and enters the feeder lane, the driver immediately feels the automatic car control take effect. As it approaches the motorway on a long sweeping curve, the car automatically accelerates to a steady 50 miles an hour, ready to merge with the continuous flow of traffic on the through lane. For a mo-

FEEDER LANES TO THE MOTORWAY   Futurama Photo by Richard Garrison

ment, the truck parallels the motorway on the feeder lane and then is automatically slipped into a gap in the outside of the four lanes provided for 50-mile traffic. There was a break in the automatically spaced line of cars which allowed him to enter. Otherwise the speed control on the feeder lane would have held the car back until a space was available. A slight delay wouldn't have bothered the driver greatly because he knows that once he is on the motorway there is never any delay. This delay would mean no more to him than that which an airplane pilot experiences when, after taking off, his plane climbs carefully and slowly to the desired altitude before getting up full speed. As a transatlantic steamer makes slow progress leaving New York harbor until it reaches the open sea lanes, it may sometimes be necessary for a car going on a long journey on the motorway to encounter a short delay before reaching the uninterrupted high-speed lanes.

Ahead of the truck, the motorway is bathed in an even glow of light; car headlights are extinguished; the driver can't help wondering how he ever found his way about in the dark benighted era when each car carried angry, stabbing lamps that blinded the other fellow. As he speeds along on a straight-line course, cutting through the Blue Ridge Mountains and the Alleghenies, he can feel the control mechanism of the motorway maintaining his truck in its lane. The nearest car in his lane is 150 feet away. On the right lies a wide right-of-way strip, beautifully landscaped. On the left, alongside the fourth lane, is a wide strip of grass beyond which he sees two more lanes of cars rushing past. They are the 75-mile-per-hour lanes. Beyond that, with another wide grass strip intervening, is the single 100-mile lane. The foliage of trees and shrubs conceals a similar eastbound right of way paralleling this westbound one. All types of motorized vehicles use this motorway—heavy trucks like the oyster dealer's, small farm trucks carrying produce to market, trailer trucks similar to a Diesel train, large and small passenger cars, tourist trailers,

HE NATIONAL MOTORWAY CROSSES THE GREAT DIVIDE WITHOUT SPEED REDUCTION Futurama Photo by General Motors double-decked transcontinental buses with comfortable lounge space. All move steadily and easily, without dust, danger or delay.

The driver presses a button on the instrument panel which will maneuver him into the 75-mile lane at the first opportunity. All the way across the country there is no danger of sideswiping or bumping or of intersections. The whole thing is managed by automatic car control. Later on, he shifts into the 100-mile lane.

He has a lot of time to look around. He notices feeder lanes from other cities leading into the motorway. But he never has to slow down for these cars to get on the motorway. Never at any time does he have to slow down for any reason. Crossroads underpass the motorway. Long-distance drivers are not the only ones to benefit from such a motorway. Local traffic flows more freely, because local roads no longer bear the burden of through traffic for which they were not designed. There are no visible lights. There are no road hogs. The motorway has taken all the irritation out of driving. The road has met the automobile at last on its own terms. The oyster dealer bought his truck for speed and reliability. The motorway has also given him safety, comfort and economy.

Midnight. The relief driver has taken the wheel while his friend sleeps—not sitting up, but comfortably, in a bed in the truck cab. Neither raucous horn blowing for a right of way nor squeal of brakes wakens him. A sign flashes, telling the driver that Chicago is 47 miles due north. He checks up on his clock; it's only 1:30. He has passed Pittsburgh and Fort Wayne without realizing it—they lie outside the route of the motorway. The shortest highway route in 1940 between Washington and Chicago was 697 miles. If he could have managed 45 miles an hour—which he could not have done because of all the cities and towns through which the highway passed—the trip would have taken at least fifteen and a half hours. It was a fifteen-hour trip on the train. But the motorway connecting Washington and Chicago is only 625 miles, exclusive of the feeder highways from both cities. Therefore, driving at 100 miles an hour while on the motorway and allowing ample time to approach and leave the motorway, the whole trip takes only nine hours.

The motorway does not actually enter either city. Its terminal points are situated so as to permit feeder roads to distribute traffic and avoid congestion.

The truck speeds westward. There is no need to slow down for the 2-mile bridge over the Mississippi or for any of the intersections with other motorway routes.

Then behind them, dawn begins to break. There is a great sight to be seen to the eastward as they fly over the great plains of Nebraska. As the morning wears on, the hot, dusty atmosphere is unbearable, but in the air-conditioned truck cab the men are cool and comfortable.

At regular 20-mile intervals along the motorway there are combination gas stations, emergency stations, restaurants and hotels. A driver always knows these facilities will be available ahead of him. At one of these points, the oyster-laden truck automatically transfers to the 75-mile lane and glides into the station from the transition lane leading to the 50-mile speed route. They stop for a light breakfast while the truck is being refueled and checked.

Speeding toward the west again on the 100-mile lane, after the short rest, through Northern Colorado and on past Salt Lake City, the driver notices a slight but barely perceptible upgrade.

Now a voice over the dashboard speaker tells the driver he is entering the Rockies.

Through the haze to westward, the first profiles of great mountains appear. It is clear that ahead are conditions which made new problems for motorway engineers. The four essentials that were built into the motorway always stay the same: safety, speed, comfort and economy. But these essentials have to be

[156]

CONVENIENT EMERGENCY STATIONS ARE LOCATED ALONG THE MOTORWAY

Futurama Photo by Richard Garrison

MOTORWAYS WILL UNCOVER MORE OF NATURE'S RICHES

[158]

handled separately here in relation to the particular demands of each of the three speed lanes.

Something happens now that they are in the foothills. Ahead is the Great Salt Lake. The 100- and 75-mile lanes draw together as the course continues straight toward the body of water. Next the westbound lanes contact the eastbound lanes of the same speeds. The 50-mile lanes, however, swing out around the lake. The two 100-mile lanes gradually ramp up over the four 75-mile lanes. All six of these lanes continue straight across the lake. The 75-mile lanes form the lower deck of a bridge with the 100-mile lanes forming the upper deck.

Across the body of water a second thing happens. The 75-mile lanes are emerging from beneath the faster ones. The increasing grade has necessitated the separation. These 100-mile lanes must rise at a lesser grade than the others in order to maintain their uniform high speed. The 75-milers veer off slightly and form a two-directional system

MOTORWAY ROUTES SEPARATE IN THE MOUNTAIN FOOTHILLS TO MAINTAIN THEIR ECONOMICAL SPEED
Futurama Photo by Richard Garrison

of their own, on a route adapted to their specific requirements.

Each of the three groups of lanes has its own speed, its own particular gradient and its established curve radius. All three factors remain constant.

The 50-mile lanes are climbing from the valley floor. They resemble the best highways of 1940—except, of course, that they are designed to maintain maximum-minimum speed and constant grade. They by-pass many natural obstacles, as the old highways do, and describe a somewhat circuitous route. The 75-mile lanes are intermediate—a compromise between the methods of the 50 and the 100.

THREE SPEEDS—THREE ROUTES   Futurama Photo by General Motors

The 100- and 75-mile lanes climb on a much straighter route than the fifties—using cuts, fills, bridges and tunnels—but still, where the terrain demands it, they give way in curves of great radius and follow the more advantageous features of the land. All curves are so gentle that they have no more effect on driving than a straightaway. The 50-mile lanes are best for tourists who want to enjoy all the beauties of the scenery, or who want to leave the motorway oc-

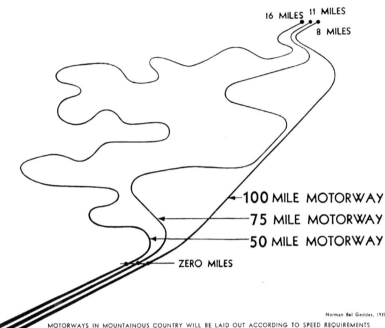

16 MILES 11 MILES

8 MILES

100 MILE MOTORWAY

75 MILE MOTORWAY

50 MILE MOTORWAY

ZERO MILES

Norman Bel Geddes, 1935

MOTORWAYS IN MOUNTAINOUS COUNTRY WILL BE LAID OUT ACCORDING TO SPEED REQUIREMENTS

casionally by means of a feeder road, to linger at one of the resort hotels. The 75-mile lanes are best for the conventional through traveler. But the 100-mile lanes are for those who mean business—those who have to get across the Great Divide in the shortest time.

Suddenly the motorway enters a tunnel. There is a surprise here. It isn't the usual dark kind of tunnel. It has been cut so close to the side of the mountain that its outer walls have openings cut into it for the admission of light and air. There is no need of headlights, no gasoline haze, no stifling air.

From the tunnel mouth, the lane whirls onto a suspension bridge straight for the next massive mountain of granite. Below to the right is the 75-mile-lane system, swinging along the upper reaches of the gorge. Considerably farther down the valley runs the silver ribbon of the 50-mile lanes. That valley down there has always been fertile but it was inaccessible until recently.

Futurama Photo by Richard Garrison

HIGH SPEED ROUTES TUNNEL, BRIDGE AND CLIMB WHILE LOW SPEED ROUTES WIND IN THE VALLEY

Now there are grazing slopes and terraced farms and newly developed lands: all made possible because the motorway has opened it up. Far away a white wisp of smoke marks a train. The air grows sharp and sparkling. The driver barely notices the steady climbing because the grade is so gradual. A cliff looms ahead. The only way to get around it would be to hang the highway upon the face of the cliff—and that is exactly what has been done.

Where the motorway runs through country susceptible to heavy snow and drifts, the road surface is of expanded metal with gratings that allow the snow to fall through, and it is treated with a chemical to melt it. In other

[162]

sections, a chemical is automatically sprayed over the road surface from hydrants along the right of way, melting and flushing the snow as it falls and preventing it from becoming packed and dry.

The next sign that blinks past tells the story: "ALTITUDE 7,000 feet."

After a short run across the roof of the world, the 75-mile route joins up again. Before long the 50-mile does likewise but it has used triple the mileage of the hundreds in the meantime. As glittering peaks drop behind them, they sail along through stands of spruce, catching glimpses of lower and lower valleys before them, until, in a vast prospect, they come out on the western margin of the continent.

By 4:45 the radio is reminding the truck driver that just ahead is a transition point where he must go through

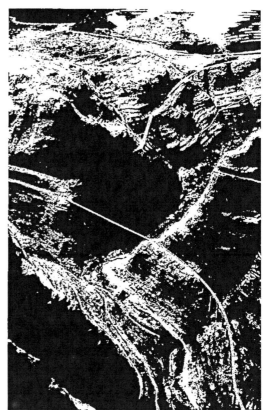

Futurama Photo by Richard Garrison

ON TOP OF THE WORLD

deceleration lanes to reduce his speed to 5 0 miles and so turn off on the feeder for San Francisco. On a wide express boulevard, automatically controlled just like the motorway, he slips into the city in time for delivery and dinner. He has traveled from the Atlantic to the Pacific, on land, in twenty-four hours!

It may sound fantastic. At least, it sounds remote. But it can be done. It won't be done all at once. It won't be done in a year's time. But it will be done. The need for quicker and safer and more economical transportation demands it. The imagination and courage of America will attend to it.

ELIMINATE GRAFT AND DOUBLE HIGHWAY CONSTRUCTION

J ust as important as the technical and physical side of highway building is the human side. Throughout the history of transportation, there has almost always been a conflict between designers and technicians on the one hand, and grafters and profiteers on the other hand. To know roads, one should go behind the scenes of road building to examine the elements of control— those social institutions and agencies which are in charge of the execution of the public's demands for quicker, safer, more comfortable and more economical means of transportation. One should know how governmental bodies work and have worked, where the money for roads comes from, where it goes and where it ought to go from now on.

Twice as much money is spent for roads today as is justified by results. This is a strong statement. But it rests on two major facts: inefficiency and graft. Of course, it is often difficult, if not impossible, to distinguish one from the other. Graft is often passed off as inefficiency. It is inevitably covered up and glossed over. The forms of graft which affect roads vary from outright robbery and bribery to more subtle forms which often go undetected. "Waste"

PORTRAIT OF ANY MOTORIST

H. I. Williams

and inefficient construction always have been and are today all too prevalent. As a result, roads cost too much to build, wear out too quickly, require constant repair and unnecessary maintenance costs.

Possibly even more ruinous than the outright theft of highway funds is the "political road"—the road routed not where it can be of most service, but where it will most profitably serve the interests of those in political authority. This practice is reminiscent of gerrymandering, a process named after Governor Gerry of Massachusetts, who in 1812 divided Essex County into a salamander-shaped district which served no purposes other than those of his political party. When Thomas Jefferson was President, he received a letter from his Secretary of the Treasury, Albert Gallatin, who urged that the national highway then under consideration should be routed through Washington County, Pennsylvania. The Secretary argued that Washington County "gives a uniform majority of about 2,000 votes in our favor, and if this be thrown by reason of this road in a wrong scale, we will infallibly lose the State of Pennsylvania at the next election." You can look up any history book and find that Mr. Gallatin's party *won* the next election. But you don't have to look up any books to find how the Old National Pike was routed. You can drive over the site of this road today—where it ran squarely through the strategic Washington County.

A National Transportation Program, published two years ago by the Transport Association of America, stated that: "In the recent Highway Cost Study conducted by the State of Illinois, it was found that that State, which has more miles of rural concrete pavement than any other, will be obliged to begin in 1938 with a program of reconstruction many years in advance of that anticipated, and for which no provision has been made. Recent studies indicate that at current prices and vehicle tax rates, all contemplated motor vehicle revenues will be consumed in annual payments against principal and interest

[169]

on highway bonds and the reconstruction of existing roads, and still leave an annual deficit of more than $6,000,000. The indebtedness in question will not be completely paid until 1957, yet much of it represents the construction of the 3300 miles of concrete roads which must be rebuilt over the next ten years. Conditions in Illinois are doubtless representative of those which exist in other States."

Unfortunately, graft and inefficiency are not new developments. Perhaps

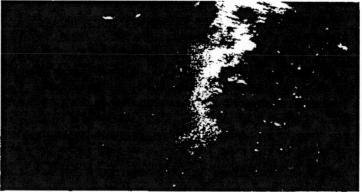

HIGHWAY FUNDS DIVERSION AND ITS ROUGH EDGES   Portland Cement Assn.

if they were, their novelty would attract the public's attention and something decisive might be done about them.

Primitive trade routes had at least one thing in common with modern highways. Both have been a means of extorting an infinite number of penalties from the hapless traveler. Rulers of states have always found highways an inexhaustible source of revenue. Robber bands, sometimes in an unholy alliance with the authorities, snatched easy profits with a flourish of a sword or the threat of a gun. There was never anything in American history which was akin to the organized robbery of the rich old caravans in Europe and Asia. But we have our tradition of stagecoach and train robberies. And the automobile highway has inherited that tradition. In Toledo, Ohio, this situation became so serious that the police, over a considerable period of time, turned off the city traffic lights after dark because so many motorists were being held up when they stopped for red lights. But this is only the most obvious form of highway holdup. Roads in America since pre-Revolutionary days have been paved with some good and many highly questionable intentions.

In 1811, the Federal government undertook construction of the Cumberland Road, from Cumberland, Maryland, to Wheeling on the Ohio River, its first big venture in road building. State interest in highways started ten years later, when Kentucky set up the first State Highway Department. Public interest in highways and Federal highway activities languished over the next fifty years, due to the interest in railroads and their development. In 1893 the Office of Road Inquiry in Washington was organized, having very few powers and acting chiefly in an educational and advisory capacity. This resulted from the resourceful crusade of A. G. Batchelder and Colonel A. A. Pope, each of whom became known as the father of good roads. Most of the interest in roads and highways during the nineties was a result of the efforts of the League of American Wheelmen and the national craze of bicycling.

At the beginning of the twentieth century there were only ten state highway departments in the country, and it was not until 1908, when Maryland established the principle that highway routes were subject to state control, and that paved highways should at least connect county seats, that there was any thought of state highway planning. In 1916, the idea that the central government had certain duties toward interstate transportation was embodied in the Federal Aid Highway Act, which provided for Federal aid grants for

[171]

road construction on condition that the states match these appropriations dollar for dollar. The immediate basis for this was the Federal government's interest in the moving of mails and of troops. Under this plan as amended and subsequently enlarged by relief legislation, over three billion dollars have been authorized by the Federal government to aid roads built under state supervision. Under the Highway Act of 1921, no state could receive Federal aid unless its highway department collaborated with the Secretary of Agriculture to frame a national system of interrelated highways.

The Office of Road Inquiry subsequently was changed to the Federal Bureau of Public Roads, and in 1939 its name was again changed, this time to the Public Roads Administration. This bureau does not have the authority to design or build roads. Its functions are simply to carry on research and experiments on all aspects of highway construction, to investigate and approve state projects, and to allocate funds, examining and supervising state highways on which Federal money has been spent.

Where do these millions of dollars expended by the state and Federal governments on roads come from? The motorist pays, and pays in full. From the moment he purchases his car, he automatically begins to supply the revenue. It has been estimated that 10 to 15 per cent of the purchase price of his car represents taxes—direct and indirect. The tax on his car and tires, registration and license fees are only his initial contribution. An enormous and continuous form of revenue derives from gasoline taxes, as well as road and bridge tolls. There is no lack of income from roads. It amounts to one-seventh of the total taxes collected by Federal, state and local governments. Yet, although one and a half billion dollars are paid by motorists in taxes each year, three miles out of every four in this country are still dirt roads.

Obviously what has been happening all along is that the motorist is not getting back, in the form of roads and their maintenance, anywhere near all the money he pays in the form of taxes. There are many reasons why he isn't getting it back. The most harmless of these is that the forty-eight state highway departments have not yet formulated a uniform accounting system. It is very hard to figure out how much has been put back into roads.

Under the present system of highway finance, little consideration is allowed for highways as one of America's most vital public utilities. The Federal government is contributing vast amounts of money to them, without the authority to plan or direct construction. Among states which are in straitened financial circumstances, there is a growing practice to divert highway funds to other uses.

Diversion might simply be called a matter of financial juggling. About twenty-three years ago the public first became aware that motor vehicle tax revenues and other highway funds were being used for "general purposes." At that time the sum involved was about $700,000. But by 1935, Congressman Cartwright, Chairman of the House Committee on Roads, charged that the diversion had reached such an extent that instead of spending all motor revenues on highway building, maintenance and the retirement of obligations, in that year diversion reached the "staggering sum" of $146,449,711. This amount of money could build 300 miles of the most advanced type of divided highways with grade separation at all crossings—more miles of this type of highway than are in existence in the United States today after thirty years of road building. Instead, over $86,000,000 of it went into general state funds, $15,000,000 into relief, $31,000,-000 to education, "and the rest into airports, oyster propagation,

[173]

Above: ONE FUEL BUT TWO TAXES
Below: IMPROVEMENTS TAKE
THEIR TOLL

GOOD HIGHWAYS HAVE BEEN BUILT   United States Department of Agriculture

etc." Congressman Cartwright summed up the situation by saying: "Wearing
the decoration of the double cross, the American motorist, some twenty-five
million of him, arises to ask why he should continue to stand for taxation
without representation—a small matter about which America once fought
a war."

Two years later, a highway engineer and President of the Portland Cement
Association, Frank T. Sheets, speaking at an annual meeting of the Greater
New York Safety Council, also charged that a high percentage of highway
funds was being misused throughout the nation. He said, "We are now col-
lecting in motor imposts (license fees, miscellaneous fees and motor fuel
taxes) about one billion dollars a year. . . . But what have we been doing

with these funds?" He explained that $147,000,000 a year is being diverted from highway use, and another $144,000,000 a year is being handed back to political subdivisions to be expended without any supervision by the states and without any definite plan.

Governor J. M. Futrell of Arkansas, several years ago, became aware that his state's highway funds were mysteriously disappearing. He flatly expressed his belief that the proceeds of Arkansas highway bonds aggregating $163,-000,000 had not found their way into actual road construction. "It is my opinion," he said, "that a fair appraisal of our roads will show a 50 per cent value of the bond issues. Properly invested, $81,500,000 would have given us a better system of highways, and, certainly, a better constructed one." The Governor did not state specifically what had happened to the money, merely remarking that it had gone "like water."

Frequently such bonds were bought by investors in other parts of the country. Local citizens were so pleased with the sudden influx of ready money that they did not trouble to count the cost. Nor did they make any effort to prevent dishonest administration of highway funds. The citizens who used and paid for the roads began to realize how thoroughly they were cheated when many miles of road crumbled after just a year of use. A report of the Highway Audit Commission of Arkansas indicated overcharges of over $4,000,-000 on one job of $10,000,000!

Economically and ethically, diversion of highway funds can only lead to disaster. The result of it is that, as Chester H. Gray, Director of the National Highway Users Conference, wrote, "States which are now guilty of diversion of highway funds see their roads deteriorating." In several states, constitutional amendments have been introduced to forbid the use of highway funds for any except highway purposes.

Then comes the large and shadowy subject of graft. Graft, after all, is just

ONE-HALF OF A STATE'S ROAD FUNDS—GONE LIKE WATER

another kind of diversion—the use of road funds not for the interest of the people, but for the interests of certain individuals.

Wastage of highway funds is a time-honored practice. As far back as 1831, Lemuel H. Arnold, a candidate for Governor of Rhode Island, was accused of instigating a fraudulent deal involving the Providence and Pawtucket Turnpike. It was charged that as members of the General Assembly, he and an associate had tried to get the Turnpike to buy up, at an inflated figure, a section of road of which they were trustees. They were further to receive a heavy annual cut of the tolls paid and were to pad their maintenance costs.

A fantastic case of graft was the grandiose scheme devised in 1871 by New

York's master corruptionist, William H. Tweed, to carve a monumental boulevard out of the wild ledges from Nyack to Hook Mountain, where a scenic hotel was to be built. Contractors grew rich on the project, but somehow they were never required to produce the road. Finally work was begun in earnest—in 1939.

The same theme, an air with variations, is heard at regular intervals in almost every state in the Union. The highway construction companies and the inducements they offer for preferred consideration when contracts are awarded are a special temptation to many highway officials. All this tends to boost building and materials costs at the start. In July, 1939, the Governor of Louisiana uncovered an instance of this and obtained the resignation of the head of his Highway Commission. Before that, it was Ohio's turn. In 1938, Governor Davey ordered Harry A. Sparks, an engineer in the State Highway Department, to be dropped from the payroll. Mr. Sparks had testified before a State Senate Committee that estimates were padded so that a ring of bituminous road material men could make exorbitant profits in selling the state the material used to produce tar roads. The state had paid $14 per cubic yard for bituminous material which the Federal government buys at $6.56! Mr. Sparks also charged that the state had wasted $2,000,000 on bituminous roads within two years. The same investigation disclosed that the State of Ohio had been charged $9,000,000 for surfacing material which should have cost just half the amount. One company testified that it had to pay twenty-five cents to an associate at Democratic headquarters for each ton it sold to the state.

These are figures on the accountants' books. They don't include the multifold unaccountable expenditures. The practice of purchasing the roads through private construction companies probably adds a few more million dollars of overcharges, extras, and exorbitant expenditures beyond a fair construction cost. The fact of the story is that the money wasn't properly spent. It bought roads that through inferior specifications and contracting lined the builders' pockets.

A recent example of highway graft occurred in the construction of Connecticut's Merritt Parkway. A report to Governor Wilbur S. Cross listed the types of crookedness that appeared there. Highway contracts were rigged. Miles of roadside graded by one highway unit were torn up by another. Cracked concrete bridges were approved. Road materials were inadequately tested, and credibly enough, the work was poorly inspected. Land assessed at about $14,000 was sold to the state by one of its legislators and members of his family for $100,000! In Greenwich, the state paid over $1,000,000 for land assessed at less than one-tenth that sum.

A land agent for the state in Merritt Parkway deals, G. Leroy Kemp, was charged with having conspired to divide commissions with two real-estate brokers representing persons who sold much of the land to the state. He was convicted. Another state purchasing agent refused to buy a piece of land at $16,000, yet paid $24,750 for the same property immediately after a woman

CONNECTICUT GETS A HIGHWAY—GRAFT UP TO 10 MILLION DOLLARS

Gendreau

had purchased it at the lower figure. As a result of this and other similar transactions, the same woman received $245,000 from the state for property acquired by the Merritt Parkway project. Notable among her real-estate ventures was the sale to the state of a house—not once but twice.

As a result of grand jury investigations, Governor Cross asked for and received the resignation of a State Highway Commissioner. After this, the land required to complete the Parkway was acquired at reasonable cost. Condemnation proceedings were effective wherever excessive prices were asked.

Nobody has ever yet attempted to figure out how much money has found its way from the highway into the pockets of grafters. Nor is it possible to estimate how many citizens are killed and maimed in highway accidents on faultily constructed or inadequate roads, the funds for which were, legally or illegally, diverted. But it *is* possible to estimate the number of people who have been victims of these modern highwaymen. The number exactly equals the total population of this country.

Because of the difficulty in detecting graft, it is also difficult to know where to place the blame for it and how to prevent it. Dishonesty is insidious; it creeps in surreptitiously even in well-guarded places. It is certain that the restraining influence of the U. S. Public Roads Administration holds a great deal of potential graft in check. Chief Thomas H. MacDonald is a scrupulously honest administrator, and he has always demanded similar quality in his associates and on all road construction over which he has had authority as a result of Federal aid. But in spite of his vigilance and the honesty of many other public officials—local, state and Federal—graft continues to thwart highway progress in many ways.

Graft, as everyone knows, cannot be prevented by constitutional amendment. It forces itself on the minds of citizens not so much because it means crime as because it means waste and inefficiency. Elimination of graft will not,

all of itself, give you an efficient highway system. But it will give you twice as much for your money.

A figure by now familiar is this: the cost to business of delay due to congested traffic runs as high as $1,000,000 a day in New York City alone. Another revealing statement is this, made by the National Safety Council: the money wasted in 1937 traffic accidents would have built thirty-five Empire State Buildings or sixty-five ocean liners like the *Queen Mary*. Such facts bring us up against the basic question: if we want a system of highways that will put an end to this appalling toll, how will we keep grafters, diversionists, and log-rollers from running off with a large share of the money?

Whatever such highways will be, they should not be laid down hit or miss by those in authority in thousands of local communities. Highway undertakings are not local enterprises, or at least should not be, because highways or any individual parts of them go to make up a complete national highway transportation system. Building small sections of highways under local jurisdiction without fully understanding the part which such highways must play in the whole national transportation network cannot produce a unified national highway plan for automobile transportation. At present the Federal government is, however, empowered to do little more than confer with local bodies, grant them money, and then erect the august "U.S." shield on the roadside, although Washington spends a sum of over $200,000,000 annually for road-building and grade-crossing elimination, to supplement the contributions of the individual states.

Efficient national highway transportation is as vital to the well-being of the American public as is the efficient transportation of mail and other similar

undertakings of the Federal government. There is a Federal obligation to develop the country's resources of land, water power, and natural wealth. And there is no single undertaking more important to these obligations than the development of facilities for national transportation.

That Federal agencies can do such work is abundantly proven, if only by the record of the Army Engineer Corps. This organization built the Panama Canal. It built, among other dams, the great Bonneville structure in Oregon. It is now building a few roads in Texas for the Air Corps. Compared to what goes on in usual highway construction, there is very little inefficiency in the Army. And as for graft—if graft were exposed and proven before an army court martial, the punishments would be so severe that they would be a strong deterrent to any further dishonesty.

Many highway authorities put forth the argument that Federal road building might be considered as part of the Federal government's obligation to develop the country. Few Federal activities are profitable in the sense of commercial undertakings which must show an immediate cash return to justify the investment. The Federal government is the only agency constitutionally responsible for general welfare in its broadest sense. The American people would not willingly break up among the forty-eight states the Federal government's responsibility for carrying the mails. They would not dispense with their Navy, or the Panama Canal, even though these maritime ventures may seem remote to most of those who dwell inland. They take for granted the purchase of an enormous and relatively isolated section of land such as Alaska, and they approve the maintenance of large public parks, such as Yellowstone, for the enjoyment of tourists. All of these are costly ventures, yet the Federal obligation to see them through seems as natural as a parent's responsibility to put his child through school. The paternal relationship requires intelligent and unsparing development of the child's abilities. In similar fashion, there is a Federal obligation to develop the country's resources of land and its facilities for transport.

Once that obligation is fully recognized as applying to the American highway system, work can begin. First of all, people will stop thinking about individual highways, laid down from here to there because of a burst of inspiration by some state or county commission. They will start thinking about an organized system of highways, laid out according to a national plan. They won't congratulate themselves on finding that this stretch or that stretch of road is being built honestly and efficiently. They will demand that kind of building from the system as a whole. They will not have to go to work throwing out and replacing a whole panel of local officials in order to get a notorious local bottleneck straightened out. Once they stop buying their roads in little chunks, from time to time, from corner dealers whose rating is often questionable, they will no longer find themselves being short-changed.

Bad roads are more expensive to travel on and to maintain than good ones. That is the argument which stands head and shoulders above all technical disagreements over "broad" versus "strict" interpretations of the Constitution, or over central versus local government. The corollary of that argument is that good roads are a sound investment. Poor roads are an economic liability.

The greatest political grab bag today for making up deficits and for padding political pockets is made up from the appropriations voted for the construction and improvement of the country's highways—the routes that are such a vital part of the nation's transportation system. As a result of this, highways are poorly constructed, are expensively constructed, are in constant need of repair, and the transportation of goods and men bears the resultant

[182]

TUNNEL ENTRANCE TO FUTURE MOTORWAY

burden. The many taxes and imposts which go to make up these appropriations are out of all proportion to the benefits received. Good highways cost money—a great deal of money—but if that money were put into their construction, instead of into oyster propagation or other similarly unrelated enterprises, the motor transportation system of this country would benefit so directly that the return would justify the investment.

MOTORWAY SERVICE TO TOWNS AND VILLAGES

WHEN a small town succeeds in getting a fine new highway put right through its center, it gets not only contact with the outside world; it gets impact, it gets congestion. The new road carries a far heavier load than the town's own traffic. A storm of cars hits the town: impersonal cars, through motorists, faces no one in town knows, all-night trucking. With them they bring noise, dirt and traffic accidents. The town gets more new neighbors than it bargained for. And most of them are not neighbors at all. They have no business with the town and regard it as just another nuisance along the straightaway.

Early in the century, the small American town was in many respects what a community should be: quiet, livable, spacious, blending with the countryside and serving as a focus for a whole rural area. The roads on which it depended had been built when the town was first developed. Its streets were really country roads, widened and lined with great trees. On shaded avenues houses stood back far enough to avoid summer dust, but not so far back that their inhabitants couldn't watch their neighbors' wagons and buggies as they

COUNTRY TOWN—OLD STYLE   Underwood & Underwood

passed. All of the streets but one or two were residential. The business area was limited, not by legislation but by volume. In many cases, the main artery for carrying on a town's commercial activities was not a road at all, but an old state canal or the local railroad branch.

On the town streets, the lone grocery wagon was often the only moving vehicle in sight. It was no traffic menace. It never even came near bumping into another wagon or running anyone down. If anyone strolled out in front of the horse, its driver pulled up or around to let him pass. And when, in turn, the driver, his work finished, ambled from the grocery over to the drug store for a soda, he never thought of going to the corner crossing or of looking to right or left for any approaching vehicle. If he met a friend in the middle of that leisurely sixty-foot-wide street, they might stop to talk of many things, but never about traffic.

When the railroad came to town, it was a great event. A "main-line" railroad through a particular locality established that locality as a coming center. Older citizens sitting around the stove in the grocery store loved to talk of how cheering crowds welcomed the first train. Today anyone who has seen a smoky and tumble-down Railroad Avenue that was once a choice residential street would think that the thousands of American towns which welcomed the railroads' entry had carried their enthusiasm to an unfortunate extreme. But at the time it was essential for those towns to make contact with the outside world. They were only too ready to grant the railroad any right of way it wanted.

Highways came into town a little more gradually. There was no autocratic corporation behind them, dictating terms. The first thing that happened was simply that the town paved "Main Street." Then the road to the next town was improved to take care of the farm produce that was just beginning to come through by trucks to the freight depot. If anyone had then told a local citizen that, by allowing a state highway to route itself through Main Street, his town was giving up its old-time privacy, he would have laughed. His town had endured isolation long enough. And if anyone had told the highway builders that by using Main Street to pass through town the highway was slowing down traffic and loosing a certain amount of its value as a means of through transportation, he would have been regarded as queer. But these two things are just what happens when a highway is routed through a town. A quiet community suddenly has to exert control over an inter-city express system. The local law enforcement officer, the constable, becomes the local traffic authority. This local traffic authority, who has never had even a serious parking problem to handle, suddenly has what is in effect a national travel problem. No matter how good his intentions may be, he is primarily looking out for the interests of his own town, not of this national travel. And tens of thousands of separate authorities, looking out for tens of thousands of separate localities, when added up together don't constitute the one great authority that is essential for the operation of an efficient national highway system. The smaller the unit of government that exercises authority over road building and control, and the more dispersed

SATURDAY IN AN UNPLANNED KANSAS TOWN

these units are, the less continuity of route and surface there is. When road building depends on local and personal whims, a four-lane highway is likely to be sent swooping through a mess of haberdasheries and then, without explanation, to peter out at the town or county line into a narrow macadam road. This naturally slows down the through motorist. It is not the only unfortunate result, however, of routing highways through towns.

R. E. Toms, Chief of the Division of Design of the Public Roads Administration, has said that from a quarter to a half of all roads built during the past twenty years are unfit for the high-speed traffic they now carry. In few instances is this more clearly shown than on the patchwork routes which connect many of our small communities. Four-lane roads suddenly converge into two. Paved roads give way to dust, and then, unexpectedly, to pavement again. In New England, a sign marking the "Edge of Dover" all too often marks off the end of human comfort until the driver has slowly jogged his way to the next sign announcing a new town's limits and another decent road surface. In Kansas, the Emporia *Weekly Gazette* recently advocated a "county unit road system" to avoid the "typical township road—a road which nine times out of ten is narrow, bumpy, unkept and in some cases unsurfaced."

Naturally the local authorities have not hesitated to try out all sorts of restrictive controls on through traffic. Forced to provide special constables to control traffic which pays no local taxes, many communities have resorted to paying the salaries of such officers with fees collected from the motorists whom they arrest. In the latest report of the Highway Safety Commission of Connecticut, it was noted that thirty towns in that state had traffic constables paid solely on this basis, and that "in some places, the number of arrests is so disproportionate to that in adjoining towns as to lead to the inference that arrests are sought by the constables to swell their income, rather than provide safety on the roads." Speed traps, designed to line the town coffers, are grossly unfair to the tourist, who has little recourse against local authority.

On the other hand, when their own constituents are concerned, local officials have been slow to put through the most necessary traffic reforms. Pedestrians are allowed to jaywalk at their own risk. Heavily traveled streets are obstructed by diagonal parking. More consideration is given to soft drink shacks and hot dog stands than to clear vision at the intersections where they spring up. Towns once so charming that they might have been a special attraction to tourists have been so disfigured by catch-penny signs that the motorist flees on, too harassed by local restrictions to stop and fulfill the exalted hopes which local merchants entertained when a highway past their shops was first proposed.

The custom of locating business where traffic is thickest dates back to the days of more sparse and leisurely transport, when it was really necessary. To-day there are still plenty of vociferous small-town merchants who, overlooking the chaos that results, insist on thrusting their communities upon the attention of motorists in the baldest possible fashion. For example, when the Bronx River Parkway Extension was run within a hundred feet of Valhalla, New York, shrubbery was planted to act as a screen between the community and through traffic. So well did the shrubbery grow, and so effectively did it serve its purpose, that the local merchants demanded that it be cut away in order to keep the town from becoming "a forgotten village." The merchants' indignation grew even faster than the bushes. They explained that "the trees just about eliminate us from the outside world. Five thousand cars often pass Valhalla every hour without seeing our Broadway, close as it is." On the other hand, in many New England communities, more foresighted residents have protested in vain against the devastation of their privacy by state highways routed through the main streets and the town center.

The argument that a re-routing of through traffic means a loss of business to a town brings up the question: "What kind of business?" It does not seem credible that the Main Street merchant of recognized wares would lose anything if the hordes of cars whose only interest is to get through and out of the town never went through it at all. On the other hand, that merchant is probably losing business today simply because of the through traffic that stampedes

A DAY OF DUSTLESS REST

FARMER DUNNE HAS PERFECTED A SIMPLE CONTRIVANCE FOR KEEPING DOWN THE AUTOMOBILE DUST ON SUNDAYS IN FRONT OF HIS COTTAGE!

FROM "LIFE," 1907

Harry L. Newman

past his windows. It doesn't stop, except for the traffic light; but it does have the effect of stopping his own regular customers from getting to him and comfortably parking near by. What has actually happened is that, in reaching out for the lunch-counter trade of tourist cars, his town has lowered its own living standard and injured its own basic trade. It has allowed a fringe of fly-by-night stands and shanties to be set up around its approaches, and in doing so has both provided itself with a roadside slum and crippled its own chances for growth. It has failed to see that the interests of local traffic are exactly opposite to those of through traffic. And on its congested and disrupted Main Street the two kinds of traffic are left to fight it out.

Furthermore, rural safety vanishes with rural peace. In 1924, the number of motor accidents in rural localities and in large cities was about the same, approximately ten thousand each. Since then the number of such accidents in rural areas and small communities has increased by more than 170 per cent as compared with a 30 per cent increase in the cities of over ten thousand population.

Roads littered with mile after mile of billboards, tourist camps, roadhouses and auto graveyards not only injure neighboring towns and local traffic, but impede the very through traffic which they are designed to attract. For example, fifteen thousand cars a day use the recently built Garvey Avenue, a high-speed artery leading out of dense Los Angeles across the San Gabriel Valley in California. But besides merely traveling on the road, these cars are hailed by countless roadside signs to stop and buy Siamese cats, second-hand plumbing, and the assorted goods of—by actual count—over three hundred mushroom businesses. Highway engineers estimate that cars parking in front of the stands and cutting in and out of traffic to reach them destroy at least 50 per cent of the highway's efficiency.

What has happened is that the relationship which should exist between road and surroundings has gone wrong—or rather, there isn't any relationship. Everyone just tries to get through as best he can, running the gauntlet of a chaos of laws and landscape. But in order to see what can be done—and how easy it is to do it—take the example of the Skyline Boulevard, another California highway, which runs south from San Francisco along the crest of the Santa Cruz Mountains, leading past commanding views of the Pacific.

Farther south, the highway skirts great redwood forests. For 80 miles, through San Mateo and Santa Clara counties, not a billboard obstructs the view. Legitimate business along the way is provided for at seven restricted points. Strict control is exercised over the appearance and location of the few types of retail business which are permitted, and shops are set back from the highway to allow their customers to park without obstructing the flow of traffic. The long stretches between these limited districts are zoned against business. There are two results to this zoning rule: first, highway investment is protected; second, pleasant motoring is promoted.

Both the American Automobile Association and the American Planning and Civic Association advocate passage by all states of a uniform highway law which would establish such control for all main highways. The value and sightliness of non-commercial property would be maintained by zoning, and new building would be prohibited within 50 feet of the road. An exception is made for wayside stands selling the produce of land immediately adjacent, but even these stands would be set back 25 feet from the road so that customers would not park on the roadbed.

The Public Roads Administration stipulates that at least 1 per cent of all Federal highway funds must be devoted to roadside development. From the old practice of holding each farmer responsible for mowing down the underbrush along his own fence and ditch, America has advanced to a point where public interest in the roadside is widespread, and government responsibility

WEAVING BY-PASSES CONFUSE DRIVERS AND SLOW TRAFFIC   Fairchild

for it is somewhat more generally recognized. One midwestern state spends over six hundred thousand dollars a season just to eliminate weed growth along its highways.

Recently built motor parkways show how much more pleasant driving can be when a positive and constructive stand is taken toward all the roadside factors. Here the road's environment is controlled, not by restrictive measures, but by the outright ownership of a right of way sufficiently wide to protect all interests involved: the motorist, the adjacent land-owners, and the state. The land on either side of the road is landscaped to conform with the local setting, increasing the pleasure of rural driving and preventing commercial exploitation of the public investment. It acts as a buffer between the stream of traffic and neighboring homes. While on the old type of highways widening is often made prohibitively expensive by the necessity of condemning new buildings which have encroached on the road, and the inflation of land values since the original pavement was laid, the parkway can easily be enlarged to take care of growing traffic. For the state always has the land.

To achieve these satisfactory road conditions, planning is first applied to the road itself, freeing it of crosscurrents and the annoyances of driving through business sections. Then planning is applied to the surroundings, in order to create a harmonious environment. The third point at which planning is applied is obviously the community itself. The outcome of establishing a fruitful relationship between town and road is that life becomes more pleasant not only for the motorist, but for the resident as well. This cannot be achieved by traffic laws. It can only be achieved by design. As long as highways pass through towns, cars will pass through towns. If the principle is to be established that fast traffic should not go through a town, this must be made physically impossible.

There are communities in the United States in which this principle has

[195]

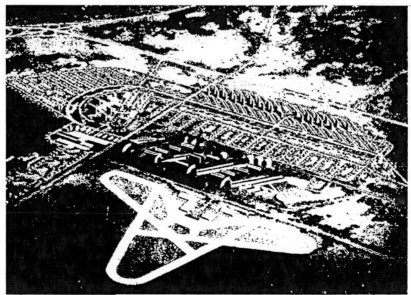

A MODEL COMMUNITY WITH FEEDERS TO THE MOTORWAY   Futurama Photo by Richard Garrison

taken concrete form. The first one of this sort was built upon plans drawn by Henry Wright in 1929, at Radburn, New Jersey. Here homes turn their back doors on the street, fronting instead on green parks and safe playgrounds inside the large residential blocks. These neighborhood units are united by a single community center, where all shopping and business can be attended to without the necessity of having to repark the car several times in front of scattered shops. Short-stop local traffic is reduced by this centralization. Through traffic in residential sections is discouraged by the discontinuous pattern of local streets. Foot traffic has its own walkways separated from moving cars by over- and underpasses. Radburn effectively shows how a community can preserve its privacy and at the same time maintain full contact

[196]

with the rest of the world. Radburn is one instance of a town that is sold to the hilt. People want to live in it. Tourists want to visit it. There is no trouble driving into it. But neither are there lines of through motorists piled up in it, all impatient and all blowing their horns.

Similar examples of town planning from the ground up are to be found at Green Acres, Long Island; Sunnyside, Long Island; Greenbelt, Maryland; Buckingham, Virginia; and Cerritos Park, California. The interest of many towns in better traffic control and better housing is shown by the recent establishment of planning agencies in Santa Cruz, California; Yakima, Washington; Sioux City, South Dakota; Waukesha, Wisconsin; North Providence, Massachusetts; Austin, Texas; Montclair, New Jersey; and the Kentucky legislature which recently passed an enabling law to permit the establishment of planning commissions in smaller cities.

Leonardo da Vinci's request that the Duke of Milan permit him to build ten new small cities in order "to separate this great congregation of people who herd together like goats on top of one another" is one of the historical instances of planning for small-town development. But the modern criterion of a "garden city" in which the best features of town and country are to be preserved was first proposed by Sir Ebenezer Howard in 1898. His ideal community, planned on a human scale, with its boundaries predetermined and its integral structure designed to maintain a balanced life, without confusion or congestion, is yet to be attained.

The idea expressed in all progressive town-traffic planning is this: Of all the vehicles on the road, only those shall enter the community which actually have business there; and of those which do enter the community, only those shall enter a given street which actually are being used in connection with people living in that street. This is becoming an ever more important principle, because as towns increase in size, sentiment grows steadily stronger against over-

BY-PASS ROUTES SAVE ONE-THIRD IN MILEAGE COST

loading the streets with extraneous traffic. What is offered as an effective solution is the "by-pass," a route to divert traffic around the town.

Studies made of cars using by-pass routes show that by avoiding the intermittent starting and stopping at city street corners, traffic can travel one-third farther at the same cost per trip. By-passes also permit the realignment of main highways so that the actual route is shortened too. They provide alternate routes in cases of emergency, and eliminate the need of costly widening of urban streets. Both local and through traffic is safer, more orderly and expeditious when the by-pass is used to segregate them. Before construction of the Keyport by-pass in New Jersey, the old route from the coastal resorts

[198]

to metropolitan areas carried as many as fifty thousand cars a day, worming their way through narrow streets and past railroad grade crossings frequently blocked by passing trains. Through traffic, once delayed for as much as two hours under these conditions of maximum hazard and inconvenience, now has a route of its own, over a two-and-a-half-mile by-pass.

Obviously it is essential that by-passes be zoned against business, and that access to them be strictly controlled. Otherwise, the route built at considerable expense to avoid urban congestion would soon be spoiled by shopkeepers shifting over to exploit it and to use every eye-catching device to stop cars which must maintain an even flow if the by-pass is to serve its purpose.

The means are available to do two things at once: first, to protect main highways from the interruptions of local traffic, and second, to protect towns from the devastating effect of through traffic. The means are available, but they have been tried only here and there. Where they have actually been used, this has been done hesitantly, piece by piece, as if people were afraid that real over-all planning would lead them too far astray from their old and cumbersome habits.

The express motorway of the future will not enter towns or even go from town to town. It will pass near to and serve the town. It will take the town's needs into consideration, as well as its possibilities for future expansion. Even the lesser highway linking two minor communities will be planned so as to preserve the integrity of both those communities. It will not clog their business areas. It will not set up competing slums along the roadsides. It will not cripple the town's chances of growth. Its purpose will be to make traffic between one town and the next easier—more safe, more comfortable, more speedy, and more economical—than it is today. It will do that first of all by segregating local traffic from through traffic. It will serve the town by means of feeders rather than by means of intersections. In no sense will it isolate the town be-

[199]

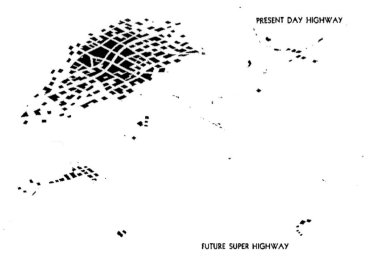

PRESENT DAY HIGHWAY

FUTURE SUPER HIGHWAY

MOTORWAY FEEDERS FROM FARM AND VILLAGE

cause it passes around outside of it. Its whole intention will be to reduce the town's isolation—to broaden its radius of communication.

Many American towns grew up in chains, each settlement about 30 miles one from the other. There was once an excellent reason why the highway should seek out the heart of each of these habitations as it trailed westward; stagecoaches needed a change of horses, passengers needed meals and a rest. According to today's range, however, these successive towns ought to lie about 300 miles apart. That is just another way of saying that it is worse than pointless for the modern car to have to stop every 30 miles just because the stagecoach once had to. The car will be benefited if it can go straight on. Driving range is constantly increasing. The range of neighbors is increasing. A time is coming when the man in the American small town will awaken to the fact that he has two communities in which to get about easily: the first, his own intimate locality, and the second, his country at large.

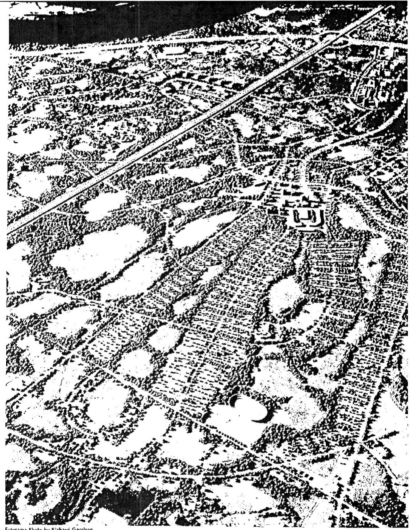

Futurama Photo by Richard Garrison

A NEW PLAN FOR FUTURE DEVELOPMENT

MOTORWAY TRIBUTARIES TO CITIES

"The Rise of Cities" is so obvious a contemporary social fact that it has become a chapter title in elementary textbooks. But, like many social facts, this one has a reverse which is also true.

Beginning with the industrial revolution, masses of people moved into cities. But now they are beginning to reverse the process and move out of the cities. From the beginning, social reformers have been begging them to get out. Robert Owen, the progressive British industrialist, in 1817 proposed that industrial workers lift themselves out of the squalor of the factory system by building small balanced communities in the open country. Fourier and Cabet designed model colonies. In the 1920's, planners in Germany, Sweden, Switzerland and other countries actually built such communities.

But historically the rebound movement from the cities has not developed by any means ideally. As the central core of the metropolis became congested, its residential advantages began to fall; rising land values rooted out its gardens and breathing-spaces; then, as Lewis Mumford writes in *The Culture of Cities,* "the original residential areas are eaten into from within, as if by

GUANO BIRDS ADOPT HUMAN HOUSING   Ewing Galloway

termites, as the original inhabitants move out and are replaced by lower
economic strata; then these overcrowded quarters, serving as an area of transition between the commercial center and the better dormitory areas, become
in their disorder and their misery special breeding points for disease and
crime." The final state is depopulation—ruined houses, no rents, no taxes: "a
vast economic and civic liability."

As people exhausted this core they began to settle on the fresh land surrounding the city. Like swarms of locusts they proceeded to devour that land,
digesting it in the form of suburbs, "developments," unplanned areas over-
built with cheap speculative housing, until these areas in turn left disorder,
blight and new slums, and people had to march out still farther. The objective
has always been to find raw land with excellent transportation into the city.
The residents want this; the real estate dealers want this; and the planners and
visionaries want it. But they have all gone about it in different ways. Most
people are far too familiar with the appearance and problems of their city's
outskirts to need any further description of what has happened. But all these
dire experiences bring home the point that in considering cities one must first

of all consider the tributary districts which lie outside and around them.

One must take into account the great popular impetus from the center outward. Great possibilities for the city lie in the land beyond it; the problem is to make that land accessible, to preserve it from exploitation that defeats its own purpose—in other words, to find a fruitful relation between city and country.

Such a relation is a problem of approaches—a problem of communication. The conventional form of development of American city transit systems is that of revolving in a vicious circle. In New York City, 85 per cent of the population is jammed into one-third of its area near the center, while the remaining 15 per cent is spread out over the remaining two-thirds. This is due to unplanned or misplanned development; to poor transit facilities at the outskirts; and the result is the cycle that leads right around again to congestion and more slums. A far-sighted planning of transit facilities twenty years ago might have made the distribution of population far more even and its transportation far simpler and more convenient. Instead of that, the city is now faced with the prospect of spending three billion dollars, not to advance its Regional Plan, but merely to make the city more livable for its present population. This is glaring evidence of past failure to plan. And even worse penalties will have to be paid in the future if planning continues to be neglected.

Certainly a basic procedure in the future should be to design transportation projects that aim at better distribution instead of merely at making the existing congestion a little more tolerable.

R. H. Macy   OTHER BIRDS DO THEIR CHRISTMAS SHOPPING

At the present stage of highway development suburban communities spread out within a commuting radius of about 50 miles from a city. That radius has lengthened in recent years in direct proportion to the increase in facilities for reaching the city. The only reason the people who go to work in the city or who produce something that is sold in the city do not move still farther out is that the present transportation system holds them in. If cars could go twice as fast as they do today, the accessibility of the city's surrounding area would increase fourfold. Assuming that the population did not increase, this would make possible a general thinning out which would give everyone freedom.

OVERNIGHT PRODUCE DELIVERY—PRESENT AND FUTURE

Such a fourfold growth of commuting area would naturally have a great effect on farm markets. Land that today is practically untouched farm country, remote from centers like New York and Chicago, would be opened up and used specifically to serve those cities, bringing in new domestic products to the cities. In New York City, where the overnight shipping radius is now 200 miles, it would jump to 500 or 600 miles, changing the entire economy.

Ever since Robert Owen's inspiration, planners have wanted to realize such a distribution. Their thought has been to regard the city as a *working* entity and the country as a *living* entity. Except in the rarest cases, their proposals have not been put into effect. But the thought has spread. The best way to break up urban congestion is to increase the radius of movement around cities. That calls for a new conception of highways planned to feed and draw off traffic.

Thus the effects of overcrowding in midtown Manhattan and the heart of Chicago are not confined to those relatively small central areas themselves. The forces of congestion originating there radiate throughout the city and affect traffic congestion in other boroughs as well as in districts out beyond the city limits. A great deal has been done, both by New York City itself and by the states of New York and New Jersey, to get traffic smoothly in and out of the metropolitan area; but the capacity and usefulness of these extensive approaches are directly dependent on the capacity of the streets of midtown Manhattan. To consider traffic problems from any angle soon forces one to consider them from all angles. To study highways means to look at the needs of rural traffic one moment and the needs of urban traffic the next. It will not solve matters to revise the system of approaches while leaving the system of city streets as it is.

The Federal Bureau of Public Roads declared in a recent report that the only way to solve the problem of traffic entering and leaving a city is to provide facilities that will carry the heavier traffic right through the heart of the city and so on out to appropriate exit points. Yet at the same time, it declared that in the case of all large cities and many smaller ones, there is need for belt-line distribution roads for other traffic.

It would seem, though, that American traffic experience has shown that when major routes go directly into cities, they cause congestion and confusion.

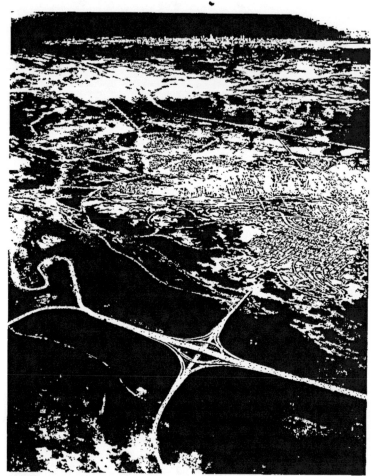

MOTORWAYS SHOULD AVOID LARGE CITIES—CONNECTING
WITH THEM BY FEEDER ROADS

[210]

When, on the other hand, they avoid cities on the Bureau's by-passing "belt-line distribution roads," they are forced out of their way, and as a result they lose a quality that is essential to a highway, namely that of being the shortest distance between two points.

Actually, there is a third alternative which makes the problems connected with both of these solutions unnecessary. It is to consider highways as straight-line routes laid out on a direct course between the environs of cities, instead of directly from the center of one city to the center of another. Tradition, true enough, calls upon the road to steer straight for the heart of town. But if the purpose of the motorway as now conceived is that of being a high-speed non-stop thoroughfare, the motorway would only bungle that job if it got tangled up with a city. It would lose its integrity. The motorway should serve heavily populated areas, but it does not have to connect population hubs directly. A great motorway has no business cutting a wide swath right through a town or city and destroying the values there; its place is in the country, where there is ample room for it and where its landscaping is designed to harmonize with the land around it. Its presence will not, like that of a railroad, destroy the beauty of the land. It will help maintain it.

The visitor to a great American city in 1960 approaches it by air, in order to see the layout of the new design more readily. It is a typical city. But it is not just any city: this one, as its towers begin to take shape far away in the haze, lies on flat terrain and along one margin of it there runs a great river. In 1940, so the statistics say, it had about one million inhabitants. The 1960 census gives it nearer two million. As one soars toward it, one's first air view is no longer that of highways becoming more and more cluttered. One misses the shabby realty developments, the marginal farms whose streams are being polluted by outlying factories, auto graveyards, dumps, and the roadside shanties that used to mark city approaches.

[211]

THE APPROACH TO THE CITY BY AIR

Futurama Photo by General Motors

All this fringeland is being held back from speculators and exploiters—held back until the day when the city's further growth will call for it. Land has been bought up for express routes which will be added to the feeders that have already been built joining the city and its surrounding land; and on this skeleton framework the future suburbs will grow.

The city makes no claim to being ideal. It was not financially possible to rebuild the city completely, scrapping its original layout. In the densest cen-

[212]

tral portion, where development and values were at their highest, there had to be many compromises. It was tough enough just to clear the worst streets there. By opening up the sections surrounding the center, by reclaiming them from misuse and blight, people were drawn out, distributing more evenly both population and traffic.

Along the feeder roads, green strips of park are laid down to prevent the tendency of industry and small business alike to spread out along the right of way and exploit it. Sometimes these strips broaden out into whole areas devoted to suburban parks and forests. Sometimes they mark the housing developments that lie outside the commercial districts in areas into which there is no intrusion. Parks have replaced the area devoted in 1940 to the ugly chaos of warehousing, shipping, and waterfront. Now they border this as a self-contained unit, with terminals, railroad yards, and a nearby housing development with recreational areas. They infiltrate into the older building mass at the city center. Smaller parks and recreation centers serve specific neighborhoods. In providing light and air, they give way to decentralization. They are not smuggled into the city plan; they are designed as integral parts of it.

The visitor's plane banks steeply over tall skyscrapers that stand widely separated in their gleaming sheaths of glass. The air terminal is about 9 miles from the city's center; this airport is interesting, not because it has been designed for 1960, but because it has been designed to accommodate all possible needs which may arise within the next fifty years after that. Its entire circular area is paved, making it possible for planes to land or take off in any direction. Hangars, service buildings, passenger facilities and buildings for personnel surround the field. At its border is a base with all equipment necessary for the handling of seaplanes.

No less than the airplanes, the railroads that enter the city are gathered together in a way that keeps them safely separate from the other forms of

[213]

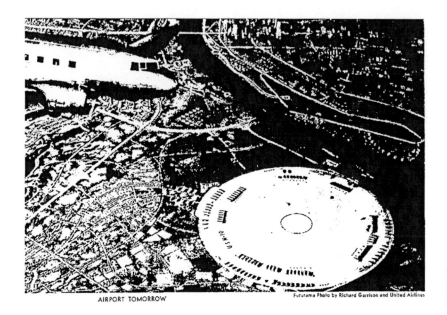

AIRPORT TOMORROW   Futurama Photo by Richard Garrison and United Airlines

transportation. They are brought underground to a great union terminal near the commercial center; then they pass under the city until at the outskirts they emerge and are redistributed in a fan pattern.

The activities of the city's docks have been coordinated in a similar central terminal.

Development of adequate transportation facilities has made such a city possible—transportation facilities which permit free flow of traffic throughout all streets within the city and, what is more important, a free flow of traffic from within the city proper to all the surrounding countryside, with adequate facilities to carry that traffic straight through a motorway system.

A network of express boulevards has been planned to provide uninterrupted traffic flow between the city and its surrounding suburbs and country facilities, giving direct high-speed rights of way to the through motorways connecting the rest of the country.

Just as the smallest village is linked to the motorway by means of convenient secondary roads, so the city is linked to it by means of high-speed feeders. These two-directional lane-segregated boulevards sweep off from the motorway in great wide curves that permit traffic to head for the city at an unreduced 50-mile-an-hour speed. Their number, width and plan are determined by the size of the city and the density of its traffic flow. The principles remain the same under all conditions. As the feeder leaves the motorway, its lanes are designed to take care of the calculated flow coming from that direction. As more commuting traffic merges with the feeder, more lanes are added. Traffic between the city proper and its outlying satellite sections moves

Futurama Photo by Richard Garrison THE CITY OF TOMORROW HAS IMPROVED ITS SHIPPING FACILITIES

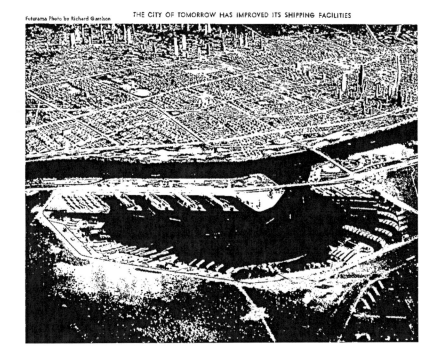

EACH CITY BLOCK TODAY IS A DENSE MASS Thomas Airviews

over these feeders, which consequently must be flexible in design. As the home-coming commuting traffic leaves the boulevards to be distributed in the surrounding sections, the number of lanes decreases so that as the feeder reaches

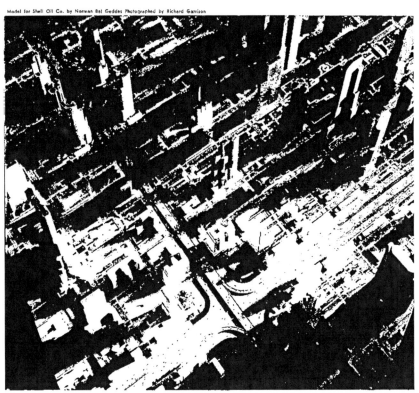

WELL-SPACED TOWERS RISE AMID LIGHT AND AIR IN TOMORROW'S CITY

the motorway, the lanes are only sufficient to care for the long-distance traffic.

Just before reaching the city itself, the lanes of the feeder boulevard fan out and form a tributary system that connects with the express boulevards within

[217]

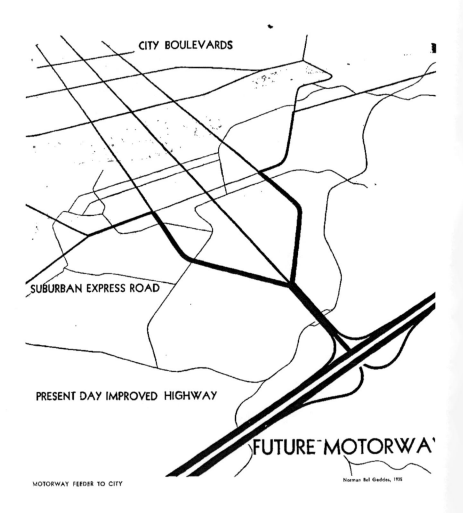

CITY BOULEVARDS

SUBURBAN EXPRESS ROAD

PRESENT DAY IMPROVED HIGHWAY

FUTURE MOTORWA'

Norman Bel Geddes, 1935

MOTORWAY FEEDER TO CITY

the city. In this outlying section there are depots, parking spaces and transfer points. Here commuters may park their cars and take subways into the business section, or they may transfer from their large high-powered rural cars and drive on in their small urban cars. Here long-distance buses transfer their passengers to small local buses. Large trucks, too, go no farther into the city than this. They haul up at loading platforms and put their products aboard city trucks or on pneumatic delivery tubes.

Thus the motorway tributary system does away with the usual bottlenecks at city approaches and hooks up, by high-speed non-stop traffic lanes, with the city's boulevard grid. However it may be laid out, one consideration is always kept in mind, and that is that the density of traffic flow both to near and far points determines the number of feeder lanes at any given point.

The job does not pretend to be complete. There are always new things to be done. But it is apparent that the city has not been redesigned for any one set of interests—either commercial or realty—or for the interests of certain individuals. It has been designed for communal use and for the means of transportation which the community uses above all others—the automobile.

ACCELERATING CITY TRAFFIC ONE HUNDRED PER CENT

Nᴇᴡ Yᴏʀᴋ Sᴛᴀᴛᴇ is more than one hundred and fifty times as large as New York City. However, between Montauk Point at the southeastern tip of the state, Lake Erie to the west and the St. Lawrence River to the north, one-third of all the miles traveled by all the vehicles in the state is traversed on the streets of New York City—within an area at most 36 miles long and less than 17 miles wide. Average motor speed in the city is about 15 miles an hour. In the center of town, on well-regulated streets, cars creep along at less than half this "speed"—at a bare 6 miles an hour.

There are, of course, a great many people in the country who do not live in New York City and who make no bones about saying they couldn't be paid to live there. Many of them, quite reasonably, prefer to consider the traffic ills of that metropolis as a localized evil which only New Yorkers need suffer—for their sins. However, it is not possible for anybody to remain unaffected by them. Throughout the nation, in one way or another, people pay toll to traffic congestion in some city where the flow of traffic is similarly hampered by channels that were not functionally designed. Something basic in America's

ONE MILLION WALKERS AND FORTY THOUSAND CARS PER HOUR

system shows itself to be out of balance. Midtown Manhattan constitutes less than 1 per cent of the total area of the City of New York, but it has 78 miles of roadway intersected by 407 street and avenue crossings. Into this area of 2 square miles every day there comes a steady influx of cars and pedestrians, hour by hour, until the peak of accumulation is reached during mid-afternoon. Then, after a short period of high tide, the movement reverses itself and humanity ebbs swiftly out. What this amounts to is that about 24,000 cars have moved in to take up the 141 miles of curb space, while some 40,-000 cars hourly try to share the right of way with nearly a million pedestrians. Result is that sometimes it takes a quarter of an hour to travel a single crosstown block. Against this rate, the 11½ miles an hour which the old horse-drawn carriages used to average along Manhattan streets is an express speed. The streets of this city, with its more than 900,000 annually registered motor vehicles, are now carrying about 20,000,000 vehicle miles daily. Three-quarters of the traffic load is carried by one quarter of the city's roadway mileage.

New York is a prize exhibit of almost everything, including sluggishness. But there are other cities with the same characteristics. Detroit, a city dedicated to automotive progress, already confessed itself stymied by the time its main industry got into full swing. In 1805 a master plan was designed to take care of the city's future growth, but in 1924 an official report said that "Detroit is being strangled for lack of sufficient circulating facilities for its

[224]

people." Unfortunately, this statement is as true today as it was then.

Pittsburgh, with its famous triangle—formed by the meeting of two rivers plus the skyrocketing of a half dozen industries—also is a trouble point. The first street plan was drawn up in 1795—when the rivers were there, but not the industries. That street plan still operates. In attempts to offset the increasing pressure of traffic flow over such inadequate thoroughfares, Pittsburgh has tried and is still trying many methods of traffic control. One-way streets, coordinated traffic signals, the limited and the restricted varieties of curb parking, street carloading platforms with and without curb cut-back for a traffic by-pass, prohibited turning movements within intersections, no stopping during the rush hours, enlarged curb radii for easier turning, and so on —in other words, splints, bandages and liniments applied to a battered traffic body.

Nor are St. Louis, Los Angeles and Chicago immune. They all suffer from the same thing: street layouts too inflexible to adjust themselves to changing conditions and growth. All three are great department-store cities. The stores settled down where the traffic was heaviest, so as to be available to the most people. And then their presence increased traffic congestion in these same areas. An exceptionally heavy burden was thrown upon the streets in the vicinity of the stores. Office buildings multiplied. In St. Louis and Detroit office buildings, the daily passenger traffic was estimated to be about four visitors for each worker. That meant still more stores and accommodations—but no change in the street plan. One suggested solution is to stagger the working hours and so ease the agonies of the rush hour. In Los Angeles a number of large concerns and government buildings have done this. This measure acts as a palliative at the peak of the crisis, but it is not a basic enough remedy to solve the fundamental problems: concentration and congestion. It is not only that the public is sadly inconvenienced by the immobile automobile, but the existence of stores

and businesses is actually threatened by it. Often, after businesses feel themselves threatened by the very congestion they have helped to create, they find
they have to move on. Industry is tending to move toward the limits of large
cities not only to escape taxes, but perhaps even more directly to escape the
cost of traffic congestion.

In New York City from the Battery to Houston Street and the upper limits
of a quaint wilderness known as Greenwich Village, streets meander now

where cows meandered before. North of a somewhat indeterminable line
bounding the "Village," near 14th Street, the city is laid out on a gridiron
pattern of rectangular blocks. Horse-cars, steam locomotives, electric street
cars and buses in turn have plied these streets. Elevated structures have been
swung above them, and subways—sometimes in two or three tiers—have been
dug under them. But in all this time the basic pattern has not changed. It has
only been touched up in details.

[226]

All over the United States the problem has been the same. It has varied only in degree.

One American city, however, did not develop haphazardly, but was laid out according to a definite, comprehensive, unified plan. Almost a century and a half ago, Pierre Charles L'Enfant was commissioned by George Washington to prepare plans for the new capital city which Congress had authorized on the banks of the Potomac. L'Enfant possessed unbounded idealism and vision. His street layout consisted of east-west streets and north-south streets upon which a criss-cross of diagonal avenues was superimposed. He could not fore-

DANGER LIES WHERE PATHS CROSS

see that the squares and circles created by this mosaic of oblique avenues would finally become at once incommodious, useless and disagreeable. When the automobile came, these squares and circles looked less and less monumental, and became more and more hazardous, until today these intersections have become one of Washington's greatest traffic problems. The elegant Dupont Circle, for example, has become a traffic nightmare. Nine thoroughfares feed directly into it. Today the District government is being forced to build overpasses and underpasses to try to break up such trouble centers.

Almost every city has its Greenwich Village and its Dupont Circle. It is likely also to have its "Master Plan," by which an expanding scheme of rectangular blocks has supposedly been laid out to last for all time to come. And it also has its Traffic Problem. This adds up to one thing: the city and its traffic have become rival elements. When the tremendous concentration of motor cars first flooded the streets, it already seemed too late to rearrange the city to accord with the traffic. So instead of that, an attempt was made to rearrange the traffic to accord with the city. The result was stalemate.

Minor rearrangements were made in the city system, of course. But such alterations were incidental, the product of immediate needs; they were not products of a general long-range foresighted plan. Cities have laid down car tracks only to have to tear them up later; they have built elevated structures and then pulled them down, tried one kind of traffic routing and then another. These rearrangements fall into two categories: first, traffic control, and second, street modernization. In order to see where they differ from real planning and where they approach it, the types must be looked at in detail.

Traffic control by means of speed laws and stop-lights is wholly restrictive in nature. City traffic is regulated by "speed" laws to the point where it barely moves at all. However, it would not be fair to say that all this control has done is to slow down traffic. If all the laws were repealed traffic still wouldn't be speeded up. Perhaps the laws have not aggravated the problem, but they certainly haven't succeeded in solving it. A newspaper report from Philadelphia, under the headline "Philadelphia Tries to Ease Congestion," says, "Continued efforts to reduce traffic accidents in this city through safety drives and traffic signal installations have resulted so far this year [1938] in a decrease of about 10 per cent in accidents and personal injuries." But this increase in safety has been achieved at the expense of speed and comfort.

Most current types of traffic control have an almost sardonic way of defeating their own purpose. Take the efforts to provide adequate parking space without adding to congestion. This problem is usually "solved" by restricting and prohibiting parking in the city and is carried out to such an extent that it is often impossible for a driver to get anywhere near his destination. The common ordinance which permits parking only for one-hour periods defeats itself because it would require more than the total existing police force of the

[228]

city to enforce it. Recently a bold step forward was taken in midtown New York. Certain crosstown streets were rid of parking entirely and then given the grand-sounding title of "express streets." But heavy trucks still lumber along them and back up in front of the doors at which they have business. Result: for the one disadvantage which these streets used to have—congested traffic—there are now two disadvantages—congested traffic and lack of parking facilities.

Other parking solutions are even more paradoxical. The city of Toledo suffered from the malignant tumor called "double parking." One would think that the cure for this ill would have been to enforce the laws against double parking. Instead, a local specialist decided that on one side of the busy streets parking should be forbidden altogether. After this was done, the drivers who had formerly double parked illegally now resorted to parking, no less illegally, right next to the forbidden curb. But authorities who felt the city's pulse claimed that the patient was improving, because now there was only one line of illegally parked cars instead of two. Another solution is angle parking, which increases the curb's parking capacity. But aerial surveys of streets

Above: TRAFFIC "FLOWING" BETWEEN CURB PARKING
Below: THE DOUBLE EVIL OF DOUBLE PARKING

in Boston showed that when allowed on average-width thoroughfares, angle parking greatly hinders the traffic flow. There is also the parking meter, which was first introduced in Oklahoma City. These meters, now in use in ninety cities, bring between three and four million dollars annually into the municipal treasuries. They are a tax. But they are not a solution to congestion.

There is one method, however, which does point the way to a future solution. It is the construction of parking space directly underneath or actually inside of heavily frequented buildings. The newest building unit in New York's Rockefeller Center, for example, is provided with six floors in which over 800 cars can find parking space by means of ramps. The same idea has been incorporated, even more dramatically, into Chicago's Pure Oil Building, in which the interior spaces of thirteen floors are reserved for tenants' cars—300 of them.

The objective is to free the streets of clogged cars. Cities must plan and build for the future in such a way that parking will no longer be a problem. Years ago it was possible to build under the whole length of Manhattan a railway system with great skyscrapers standing on top of it. Would it then be any less possible simply to build garages under buildings? The whole picture of urban congestion would be changed if apartment houses as well as great office structures provided underground space, first to accommodate tenants' cars, and second, to make it possible for trucks to load and unload off the street within the building line. Given off-street parking space, transportation cannot but become quicker and more flexible. If maximum flow of traffic is to be attained, an adequate highway is no more important than an adequate motor

ROCKEFELLER CENTER PARKING—1938  Underwood & Underwood

ROCKEFELLER CENTER PARKING—1940.
SIX FLOORS IN NEWEST 16-STORY BUILDING

ROCKEFELLER CENTER PROVIDES UNDERGROUND DELIVERY

CHICAGO TRIES VERTICAL PARKING

Ewing Galloway

KAUFMAN'S CUSTOMERS PARK THEIR CARS IN PITTSBURGH

Lehigh Portland Cement

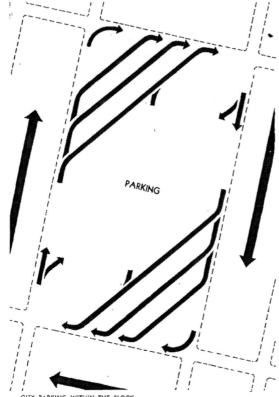

PARKING

CITY PARKING WITHIN THE BLOCK

terminal. It may well be that the next great building job for the American city will be to provide these terminals.

In addition to parking restrictions and regulations to relieve traffic congestion on the city streets, the widening of city streets to increase their capacity has been tried. In 1908 the sidewalks of the then dominant section of New York's Fifth Avenue (25th to 47th Streets) were slashed to make it possible to widen the street from 40 to 45 feet. The upper section later followed suit. It was a good solution at the time, and opened up the avenue to the great stores and buildings that crowd it today; but it led to a dead end. Today Fifth Avenue is twice as congested as it was in 1908, and there is no more room for widening. The saturation point has been passed.

All over the country, main thoroughfares copied Fifth Avenue's example. But in so doing they also copied Fifth Avenue's later history: a saturation point was reached, while on the other hand the automobile factories had not come near reaching their apex of production. City authorities, trying to ac-

NEW YORK'S WEST SIDE HIGHWAY AFFORDS TWO DECKS FOR CARS

commodate traffic where no accommodations exist, have next resorted to the one-way street. The one-way express street is an extension of this ancient idea. After that the next step is the express highway through or around congested districts—such as Chicago's Outer Drive and New York's West Side Elevated Highway and East River Drive.

These innovations give hints of what could be done in the future. Already several city authorities have gone on from the stage of finding individual solutions to individual street problems to the stage of drawing up an over-all project to relieve an entire city. An idea brought forth for crowded Los Angeles is nothing less than a network of motorways whose segregated lanes will be reached by ramps and which will bridge every intersection. In business districts a 100-foot right of way is to be acquired. On that a special structure is to be erected. The first and second floors of this building are to be devoted to retail business; the third to the motor road; the fourth and fifth to parking space; and the floors above to offices. The author of this plan is the Engineering Department of the Automobile Club of Southern California. And the purpose of the proposal is prosaically stated: "to increase property values and raise the efficiency of the automobile to close to its rated capacity."

Another plan, devised by Ernest Flagg in 1927, divided traffic into three categories: pedestrians, fast vehicles and slow vehicles. It proposed the building of elevated automobile runways providing a special right of way for rapidly moving vehicular traffic. Under these runways parking space would be available for standing traffic. All present sidewalks would be narrowed and new ones would be created at the present third-story level of the buildings. The buildings themselves would be set back 25 feet from the street at the third story, thus giving more light to the buildings and street. Mr. Flagg realized that an entire city could not be rebuilt in this way, but he asserted that every new building could be designed so as to permit the ultimate accom-

Futurama Photo by General Motors

PEDESTRIANS AND MOTORCARS WILL CONTINUE ON THEIR WAY WITHOUT INTERFERENCE

AIR, LIGHT, SPACE—AND SAFETY FOR PEDESTRIANS AND MOTORISTS IN TOMORROW'S CITY

plishment of his plan on an extensive scale throughout most of the city.

The essence of both plans is simply that the various categories or directions of traffic should be segregated. Traffic coming in opposite directions must be completely separated. Express highways must be built through congested centers to completely separate through traffic from slow local traffic. Pedestrians and cars must be kept apart—really apart. It isn't enough that the pedestrian be separated by the mere height of a curbstone from the cars which he impedes and which menace him. He must be put out of harm's reach. The pedestrian must be made into an efficient transportation unit too.

So far, the pedestrian-versus-automobile conflict has been "solved," not by making things better for both types of traffic or even for one at the expense of the other, but by making both groups take turns being delayed at street corners. The inevitable result is that neither is satisfied, and a growing antagonism has developed between them. It can only be corrected by having the pedestrian walk on a separate level all his own.

To sum up: daily experience is showing the American people that motor traffic has bogged down; that traffic "control" has meant well but solved nothing; that "improvement" and "modernization" are fine sounding words, but

THE AMERICAN NATIONAL SPORT IS DODGING A CAR

Acme

mean less and less as the facts of traffic crowd them. There is not much chance left for tinkering. The plain fact is that there is simply not enough room in cities, under present conditions, to accommodate the traffic.

One answer, and the simplest one, is that there are too many cars. Perhaps there is no need for private cars to come within certain congested areas of a city. Many passenger cars driving in a city come from suburbs, and it would be more practical for these people to come in on a subway system. Provision of clean, comfortable subways in which anyone is willing to ride would help cure this situation. Underground transportation should be made just as pleasant as travel in the present-day air-conditioned trains, and it could get people into the heart of town much faster and more economically than they could drive themselves.

The urban motor car will undergo radical changes in the future. Private cars will form a smaller part of city traffic in proportion to the large number of smaller, cheaper taxis. The wheel base of all city automobiles will be re-

SIDEWALKS ELEVATED TO SECOND STORY LEVEL WILL DOUBLE TRAFFIC FACILITIES

Futurama Photo by Richard Garrison

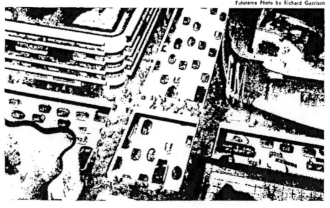

duced. Thus they will be easier to maneuver in traffic. Buses will be smaller and faster. These conveniences all combined will make it unnecessary for the 1960 New Yorker to bring his high-speed rural car into the heart of town.

In the preceding chapter, the American city of 1960 was looked at from the air. That first reconnaissance flight showed the feeders which served the city and the approaches which insured its future growth; it revealed certain broad divisions which broke the city down into the separate functions—living as against working, manufacturing as against moving, and so on—and it gave hints of the great rebuilding that had been going on. Additional details are uncovered when one comes down closer to view the great city. The observer is aware that as this grand plan is being worked out, many aims are being realized. But for the time being there is just one detailed aim which interests the observer. It is this: to see traffic in the city of 1960 sped up by just about 100 per cent.

The greatest blight area of the 1940 city occurred along its unstudied fringes. The greatest crowding occurred at the over-developed center. In 1960 both sections have been entirely replanned together—the first built up, and the second built down. Upon both there has been imposed a unified grid system of city blocks. The width of streets from building line to building line has not itself been altered; but the most apparent big change is that each 500-by-250-foot block is a complete unit in itself.

The majority of these blocks are made up of low five-storied structures. About every

PEOPLE SAUNTER ABOVE—CARS SPEED BELOW

Futurama Photo by Richard Garrison

EXPRESS BOULEVARDS ARE THE MAIN ARTERIES FOR THROUGH CITY TRAFFIC

tenth block consists of one huge skyscraper—a steel and glass shaft reaching high into the air, set back with gardened terraces and separated from the next great tower by at least two blocks of large green park, a shaft which is built around a service and elevator core so that every rentable space has the maximum of light and air. Buildings are restricted to seven different heights. Adjacent to

[240]

the buildings are recreational and rest facilities, annexes to the great sky-scrapers. Some lower buildings cover only part of the block, leaving the remainder to be landscaped. Parks cover one-third of the total land area, taking up entire blocks and groups of blocks.

Looking at the streets themselves, there is revealed at once the main principle under which they operate. Pedestrians and automobiles are kept entirely apart. The crowds of shoppers are walking on sidewalks located at the second-story height of all buildings. At intersections, they bridge the streets. Store display windows are on two levels: sidewalk and street. The windows on the upper level are designed to attract the strolling window-shopping pedestrian, while those on the lower level are of a broader, more spectacular type, designed to catch the eye of the motorist driving by. Upper building entrances make it

PARKING AND UNLOADING WILL BE REMOVED FROM THE STREET TO WITHIN THE BUILDING AREA
Futurama Photo by Richard Garrison

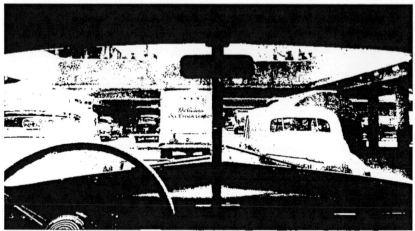

TRAFFIC LANES ARE FROM BUILDING LINE TO BUILDING LINE   *Futurama Photo by Richard Garrison*

unnecessary for the walker ever to shift to the lower level except when he wants to get his car or·jump on a bus. Then ramps and escalators take him down.

This lower motor level is no wider than was the 1940 street together with its sidewalk; but its traffic capacity is double that of the 1940 street. In the first place, its traffic lanes extend from building line to building line, not from curb to curb. Secondly, parking is done not in front of the buildings, but only within them. Third, room for turning into traffic as well as for loading and unloading is provided entirely within the buildings. None of the functions of the building encroaches upon the thoroughfare. The whole street level of the building has been cleared and opened up to become a terminal for automobile traffic, providing delivery and parking facilities for all requirements of the building without impeding the outside street traffic, as well as providing

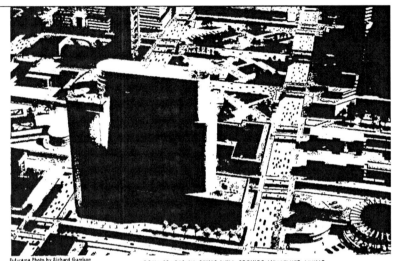

OPEN SPACES IN CITIES WILL PROVIDE HEALTHIER LIVING

elevators to the various car parking levels, waiting rooms for passengers, escalators to the sidewalk levels, and the like.

The streets themselves are all one way and of only two widths—100 feet
and 80 feet. Their regulation speed is 30 miles an hour. Where several blocks
are joined to form a park at street level, the streets ramp under them so
that there are no breaks in the flow of traffic. This city grid is again crossed,
at intervals of ten blocks each way, by a grid of express boulevards. They are
one way also and are 100 feet wide, but since they are designed to ramp alter-
nately above and below the cross-streets in a basket-weave pattern, they permit an uninterrupted, sustained speed of 50 miles an hour right through the
heart of the city. Their turns at intersections are built along the lines of the
motorway—the principle being always to maintain uniform speed and never
impede the flow. They are reached by parallel feeder streets from which ramps

[243]

lead up to them as the cars accelerate from 30-mile local street speed to 50-mile express boulevard speed.

In 1940, street speed in the great city averaged about 15 miles an hour. Boulevard speed averaged about 25 miles. By 1960 both speeds have been exactly doubled. This doubling will involve a vast original building cost. But, as Robert Duffus says, "It is the absence of a plan, not the existence of one, for which a city or region should feel apologetic on purely financial grounds. The cost of doing only what is necessary to enable a city to function efficiently, once it has fallen behind in meeting the needs of the inhabitants, would probably stagger us if we could correctly estimate it. . . . The sound city plan is first sound economically. It recognizes that a city cannot continue to exist as a civilized entity unless it earns social and economic dividends for its inhabitants." If we don't plan today, we shall pay tomorrow.

We face an inescapable choice between planning and chaos. Our sprawling, tangled cities must be transformed. Our city streets must be redesigned. Just

A TYPICAL EXPRESS BOULEVARD INTERSECTION AND FEEDERS   Futurama Photo by Richard Garrison

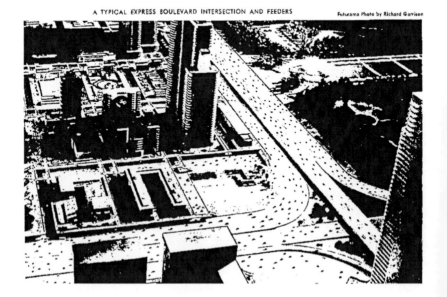

as it is time for us to start replacing the forests which we have over-cut, it is time for us to let light and air into the cities which we have over-built. The cost will be great, although engineering studies made for the city of Chicago have proved that elevated highways can be designed at a cost much lower than that of street-widening projects. It is impossible to speed up city traffic by one hundred per cent, at this stage of the game, on a pittance. Twenty years ago the cost would have been much less; twenty years from now the cost will be much greater. But the cost of failure to do so will be greater still. No city can afford the stagnation toward which many are heading.

Hope for the future lies in our determination to rebuild and redesign our cities to prevent the evils which have accumulated as a consequence of lack of planning. The success of the design, physical structure and economy of our future cities will depend on the enterprise and vision which we show today.

THE NEED FOR INCREASED DISTRIBUTION

13

FORWARD-LOOKING highway planning affects every person in the country, whether he drives a car or not. It reaches into every section of the country: rural regions, towns, suburbs and cities. Without good highways, these sections become unhealthily isolated and ingrown.

As far back as 1807 Albert Gallatin declared that in order "to unite by intimate community of interest the most remote quarters of the United States" what was needed was fast and easy communication throughout the country. As a safe and sound Secretary of the Treasury, Mr. Gallatin was no wild-eyed visionary. What he spoke was good common sense, as true today as it was then. His proposal was simply that money received by the Federal government from the sale of public land be used to finance the construction of highways and canals. That, however, did not sound like common sense to the people of 1807. It sounded like a violation of the Constitution. The cautious Jeffersonians in power could never repeat often enough the clause which reserved to the several states all powers not specifically granted to the Federal government. They interpreted the founding document "strictly." As a result, the

[248]

Federal government was prevented from making direct improvements within state borders—save for the purposes of navigation in harbors, coastal waters, and the Great Lakes. Mr. Gallatin's plan went on the shelf.

A century later there was another man in high office who was given to thinking in large terms about the needs of the nation. Theodore Roosevelt, by no means a "strict constructionist," dug a canal. For that he was regarded as dangerously rash—almost a public peril. All he had really decided was that Atlantic and Pacific shipping needed to be linked, and that the Federal government was manifestly the only agency that could do it. He also decided that since the Federal government was putting up the money, it should control its investment and run the show.

Suppose that Theodore Roosevelt, inspired as he was by conceptions of a national destiny, had applied the Panama Canal type of thinking to the American land itself, and declared that a system of direct highways was needed, no less than a waterway, to "unite by intimate community of interest the most remote quarters of the United States." There would have been strenuous opposition, but Roosevelts thrive on opposition. And the idea might have penetrated to the American people that all they had done so far in the way of road building was to lay out a patchwork crazy quilt entirely without design. They might have learned right then that roads could be planned as one great system, and that such a system could have the effect of developing the country in line with its natural resources. The results today would be of incalculable value. The nation's roads today would be a very great national asset. The advantages of the new automobile could have been set to immediate use.

But right there was the hitch. The automobile was still new. Not even Theodore Roosevelt had any idea of the possibilities of the motor car and of its coming significance to civilization. So money for road construction went on being spent the same old way.

Since Theodore Roosevelt left office, over a half million miles of highways have been built in the United States. In his day, only 7 per cent of the existing roads were surfaced with anything better than gravel. Even today there are only about 25 per cent which have hard surfaces. It is interesting to reflect that if all the mileage that has been laid down and all the money that has been spent on roads, since the first Roosevelt's day to that of the second, had been laid down and spent on the basis of a *plan,* this would be a vastly different country today. But although more than thirty years have elapsed, there is still no plan for a national highway system. Roads are still not laid down in sparsely populated sections in order to "unite remote quarters." In 1940, roads are laid down primarily between large centers. When "highway improvement" is undertaken, the usual procedure is to examine certain stretches where there are already many people, many roads and heavy traffic, and then to build more roads there to facilitate that traffic. This only results in encouraging still more traffic between these already heavily traveled and densely populated centers; and the final spin of the vicious circle leads from concentration of population and traffic into over-concentration.

At the same time there are vast sections in the United States which remain underpopulated, isolated and under-developed. This unexploited territory is often valuable, potentially very useful. It includes some of our most beautiful land. But it is just out of the way. Roads can be built to correct this situation. But, to put it simply, as road builders we Americans have failed to see the relation that exists between the transportation facilities we are building and the population trends and economic changes that may re-

FOUR LANES POSSIBLE—TWO IN USE

sult from them. We have failed to regard roads functionally, creatively.

The railroads did not stop at serving already-established population east of the Mississippi. They took the population out beyond the Mississippi. They knew that corn and grass lands were waiting there, that all that was needed was good men to farm them. They knew that if men were taken out there, they would soon create produce, and that the railroads would prosper by carrying that produce eastward. Therefore the railroad sent its rails out ahead of the population. But highways have always followed the population.

Today America has left the stage where hasty road building in the wake of an increasing population is necessary. Does not that also mean that the highway should leave the stage where it is merely passive? Highways can be made to serve a creative function. Because of the fact that in some sections of the country there is great overcrowding while in others there is great open space, new shifts in population are highly desirable. It is possible today to lay down roads in advance of this population movement, and so take a hand in determining it.

A traffic-flow diagram indicates the proportionate extent to which highways are used by the varying width of its lines. On a national traffic-flow map, the Eastern part of the country is covered with wide lines, showing that there are many roads carrying heavy traffic. Here, therefore, the major problem confronting highway planners is to relieve congestion of population and traffic. West of the Mississippi the lines are few and thin, meaning that roads

Portland Cement Assn.　　　ONE OF CALIFORNIA'S MODERN HIGHWAYS THROUGH THE MOUNTAINS

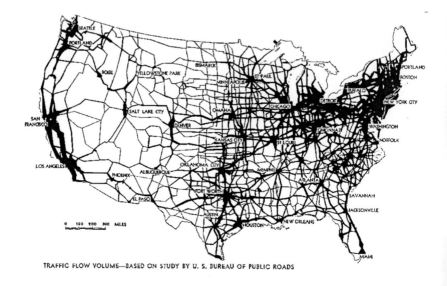

TRAFFIC FLOW VOLUME—BASED ON STUDY BY U. S. BUREAU OF PUBLIC ROADS

are proportionately few and the traffic light. Here, therefore, the problem is to develop the land. The Western area of the United States is by no means unfavorable to life. It is studded with health and pleasure resorts. Its scenic attractions are exceptional. Water for agriculture is becoming increasingly available as a result of dam construction and water control. Irrigation is more dependable than rainfall. America's greatest potential hydro-electric power reserves remain to be harnessed in the West; its largest forest reserves are also there; the natural wealth is immense.

The United States has not reached the point, already passed by many nations, at which the total population becomes static. In the past twenty years its population has increased by more than 20,000,000. By 1960 it is estimated that the total population will have increased by another 15,000,000.

MOST HEAVILY
TRAVELED 3,000 MILES

MOST HEAVILY
TRAVELED 8,000 MILES

MOST HEAVILY
TRAVELED 15,000 MILES

DERIVED FROM STUDY BY U. S. BUREAU
OF PUBLIC ROADS OF AVERAGE DAILY
TRAFFIC VOLUME

Concentration is also increasing. The great cities are growing greater. Greater New York, which today has more than 13,000,000 inhabitants, will have, it is estimated, 16,000,000 by 1960. Along with this increase in growth is coming an increase in movement. People move about more freely than ever before. Motor traffic is expected to double in the next twenty years. The radius of traffic is also growing. In the East congestion is rapidly growing to the saturation point. To break up that congestion it is necessary to open up new ways out, to decentralize, to redistribute, to create breathing-space— that is the coming need. It is a need that can be met first of all by a national highway policy.

Over and beyond the inefficiency and obsolescence of highways, there are other factors which hold up the movement toward free national distribution. One of these is local or sectional conflict —more exactly, the short-sighted rivalries between certain states. These hurdles have been placed directly in the path of a vital and growing American industry—trucking. They damage not only this specific industry, but all aspects of national distribution. Lack of cooperation between the different states, and worse, active antagonism between them, threaten to stifle interstate commerce.

Sixty per cent of all automobile traffic is for business purposes, according to the official road publication of the Federal government. In many sections of the country this is held up by all sorts of petty, conflicting state restrictions. Each state has enacted its own codes governing the permissible sizes and

[253]

weights of vehicles. Different states have piled up a host of restrictions: Iowa requires trucks to show three green clearance lights; the neighboring Missouri requires trucks to use no clearance lights. Such technicalities, costly to operators, bewildering to drivers, have in many cases been put on the statute books through pressure brought by other transportation agencies. They create barriers at state borders. A dozen state lines have "ports of entry" similar to national customs offices. Only the extra imposition of state import duties is needed to make of the entire country a jumble of forty-eight separate sovereign countries as far as highway transport is concerned.

The Constitution of course prohibits the levying of any such duties. But in certain cases what might be called "border wars" literally paralyze highway commerce. In 1932, for example, an Indiana State officer said: "We find something wrong with almost every Kentucky truck and are arresting almost 100 per cent of the Kentucky truck drivers."

These restrictions are as costly as they are silly. The Federal government contributes funds liberally for the construction and maintenance of highways. Therefore it has an interest in the whole national highway system. Over and beyond that, it has a responsibility toward national defense, and the furtherance of interstate commerce. Should state barriers across these roads be allowed to interrupt this interstate commerce?

Many persons and groups have asked that the Federal government boldly take a more direct part in highway building, in order to increase national distribution. National organizations such as the American Automobile Association, the Highway Research Board of the National Research Council and the American Road Builders Association, have carried on studies and research. A great deal of this work, though, has only scratched the surface and has not come down to the fundamental question of deciding what should be the basis of a national system. That the frame of mind of the nation today is sym-

FROM "LIFE," 1907

pathetic to some such system is proved by the fact that besides the highway plan proposed last year by the Chief of the United States Bureau of Public Roads, two bills providing for such plans have been introduced into recent sessions of Congress.

THE NEW SPORT

"THE FARMERS OF MARGARETVILLE, N. Y. HAVE FORMULATED A NEW 'UNWRITTEN LAW' FOR THEMSELVES. THEY HAVE DECLARED THAT ANY MAN MAY OPEN FIRE UPON A SPEEDING AUTOMOBILE AND TAKE ALL LEGAL CONSEQUENCES."

Harry L. Newman

Under the Bulkley Bill, introduced in 1938, a United States Highway Corporation would be created, which would build and maintain a gridwork of ten national superhighways as straight as modern engineering could make them and with the most modern safety design. Three of these would run east and west, crossed by seven running north and south. Each highway, made up of from four to twelve separate lanes, would be built on strips of property at least 300 feet wide. Additional land would be acquired along the right of way under the procedure known as excess condemnation. The value of this adjoining property would be raised by the construction of the superhighways. The plan's sponsors believe that part of the cost of building the superhighways could be met by the resale of this land.

Representative Snyder's bill, introduced in 1939, provides for the construction by the Department of the Interior of nine superhighways, totaling about 16,000 miles. This plan, basically very similar to the Bulkley plan, is still pending before Congress. Each highway would be 100 feet wide on a right of way 500 feet wide. The highways would not pass through any cities or towns unless there was no other place for the road. In case of an established

[255]

FRONTIERS FOLLOW THE ROADS—OLD SPANISH TRAIL IN MEXICO Underwood & Underwood

and improved highway already existing anywhere near or parallel to the proposed highway, it might be widened and taken in as part of it, provided it had been built to the proper specifications. The question as to whether or not these highways would be toll roads has not been decided.

The Bureau of Public Roads, under the direction of Thomas H. MacDonald, was directed by the Federal Highway Act of 1938 to investigate the feasibility of building three superhighways running east to west, and three running north to south, with an approximate total length of 14,300 miles. The routes were to be planned in relation to population distribution and were to pass through as many states as possible. Finally, subject to all previous considerations, the routes were to be located to achieve the largest possible tolls.

In working out their plan on paper, the Bureau located the proposed highways entirely on new lines apart from existing roads, in all but two sections. It was recommended that the chosen locations by-pass cities and towns, but pass sufficiently close to them wherever possible to attract their traffic. The roads were laid on a right of way which varies in width from a 300-foot minimum in rural areas to a 160-foot minimum in urban areas. Seventy-five per cent are two-lane highways situated over on one side of the right of way to allow for additional lanes in the future. The rest are four-lane highways with a center parkway strip.

After laying out specifications for such superhighways, and determining their routes, costs and expected traffic volume, the Bureau reported that such superhighways could not earn the cost of their maintenance through toll collection, and were thus not economically justified. As an alternative to the building of toll superhighways, the Bureau then presented what it terms a "Master Plan for Free Highway Development." This plan suggests the building of a gridwork of inter-regional highways. Wherever possible, these highways are to embody alignments and improvements of already existing roads. In choosing revised location, the controlling thought was to provide reasonably direct connection between major cities. The routes should enter and traverse all large cities by means of adequately designed facilities. Wherever necessary around large cities, limited access belt lines should be provided. The Bureau's plan calls for a total of 26,700 miles.

All of these proposals show a tendency to link city to city in an arbitrary grid, which will act primarily as a palliative for present traffic ills rather than as a preventive for the future.

The problem can be permanently solved only by better coordination between traffic and the needs of the population. It is not enough to consider

BULKLEY PLAN FOR SUPERHIGHWAYS—1938

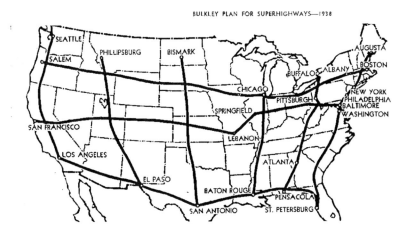

present requirements; future needs must be anticipated. Congested highway areas must be redesigned. The national traffic-flow map of the future must show a more even distribution. Every day it is postponed the cost increases.

The great public interest in national highways, and the number of proposals which have been made, have a reverse side. Unanimity of national opinion on any subject would be too much to hope for. There are a few organized groups in this country which fight relentlessly not only against projects for motorways, but even against the principles behind them. At a business meeting a few years ago, the president of a leading railroad company is reported to have said: "It is to the interest of our railroad that the highways remain congested. If there is anything which we can practically do to increase that congestion we will do it. There may be a need today for a through highway for motor cars . . . but we will oppose any such plans and will block the materialization of any such highway, just as many years as we can. If the public don't like the congested highways, let them ride the railroad."

Undoubtedly this attitude is not held by many people. The day of ruthless competition and bitter rivalry in the field of transportation is drawing to a close. By 1960, old feuds may be settled and all the energy and time which used to be given to destructive warfare may be devoted to the single purpose of perfecting our transportation and communication for the benefit of those who are most concerned—the people.

It is not sufficient to give up the present local method of hit-or-miss road planning, and substitute for that a method of building a lot of big roads on a grand scale. For the present travesty of planning, *real* planning must be substituted. Road building as it is being done won't free the country from the likelihood of future congestion. But road building as the result of a comprehensive plan to increase national distribution, eliminating local whims and fancies, ending aimless duplication of effort, taking in all the contingencies

Futurama Photo by Richard Garrison   AIR VIEW TO NEW HORIZONS

of the nation's geography, economics, and population trend—that is a very
different thing indeed.

The existence of vast stretches of "waste land" in a nation where metropolitan real estate sometimes sells for as high as $845.00 a square foot indi-
cates a lack of balance which must be remedied. And the present time seems
auspicious for such a remedy. Free trade between nations has been made im-

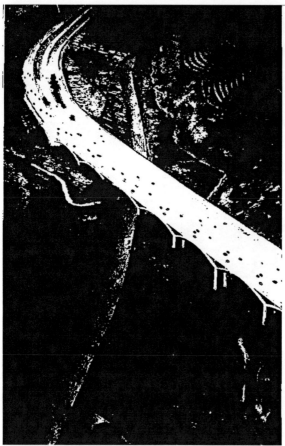

MOTORWAYS FOR INCREASED DISTRIBUTION

possible for the present. We must develop our internal market. For this, waste land is no more tolerable than is inadequate transportation.

A planned highway system would take people from points of congestion toward the unexploited lands of the West. The Interstate Commerce Commission reports that of 125,000 communities of appreciable size in this country, 45,000 have either no rail service whatsoever or lack a freight station. They rely entirely on highways for their contact with the outside world. Six million farms, with a total normal production value of about twelve billion dollars, depend upon public roads as the only means of distributing their produce. Without those roads, there is no distribution. Where the highways of a national system go, commerce and higher land values and free movement will go. Increase a country's roads, and you increase its wealth.

THINKING FOR OUR GRANDCHILDREN

THE American people are rich in many things. Above all, they are rich in union. Look at any of the empires of the past; in none of them did so great a number of people live together on so wide a land. In none of them did they enjoy such freedom and security. To all the things which Americans inherit, this union is the key. They inherit the rich, varied traditions of racial groups from all over the world which are now slowly fusing into a new amalgam, free of national and sectional antagonisms. They inherit these people's energy and belief, the fruits of their labor and the accumulation of their capital. They inherit almost every natural resource known to man and the knowledge of how to use these resources. A technology has been placed into their hands which surpasses anything dreamed of in other days. "Nothing that a people could want," Walter Lippmann wrote in his *Life* article, "The American Destiny," "nothing that nations fight to obtain, nothing that men die to achieve is lacking, nothing except a clear purpose, and the confident will to make the most of all these things."

To that union a special strength is given today by the newness of easy communication. It is a fact of importance that this is the first generation to have at its fingertips every possible means of mechanical transportation: travel on the ground, under the ground, in the water and under the water, and in the air. For the first time in history, man is now able to communicate with any point in the world, using telephone, telegraph, radio and now television. He can go any place or get in touch with any place. In this fact lie great potentialities. But there also lie great responsibilities.

The scope of men's lives has always been determined to a great extent by their facilities for movement. Without a highway system, for example, men were limited in their reach to an area of about 50 miles around them. Their whole point of view, their form of statehood, their trade and their philosophy differed entirely from that of men who were able to move out of their valleys and widen their horizon.

Whole civilizations have grown up and flowered along the lines of trade routes, and have withered when those routes were superseded by others. By means of travel and transport all the human cultures—from cities to states to nations to groups of nations—have gathered their cultural heritage or distributed it. But in all previous areas—when maps were faulty or ships inadequate or mountain passes dangerous—there was a great margin of the un-

EXISTING FARMS WILL QUICKLY ADAPT THEMSELVES TO SPEEDIER TRANSPORTATION
Futurama Photo by Richard Garrison

known. It was hard to plan. So many factors could not be determined. There were still so many immediate things to be done to make life more tolerable that perhaps it was just as well not to look ahead too far. All the people of the world stood surrounded by rings of uncertainty.

Modern communication and transportation have pierced to a great extent these rings of uncertainty. The margin of the unknown has been reduced. Men begin to see how their living conditions compare with those of people far away, to interchange experiences, correlate findings, make use of new ideas. No one in his senses would claim that today uncertainty and danger have been banished from the world. In Europe it is tragically obvious that facilitated transportation and communication do not inevitably increase harmony between peoples. In fact, when these mechanical instruments are placed in the hands of rival nations, they increase and hasten conflict. But in America, where almost a whole continent is united indivisibly, the technical inventions in the fields of transportation and communication serve a constructive purpose.

Our generation has seen a basic revolution in transportation. It has taken thirty years. We stand now at the point where this major change has been completed. What is done in transportation in the future will consist of adaptations of experiments already proven, or of further developments in means that already exist. In this respect, our generation is at a particular vantage point. It can look back upon a vast task that has just been accomplished. It can look ahead and foresee to some extent the natural results of all this—the effects that such a change will have on future generations, on our grandchildren.

In 1960, if transportation in America continues to advance as it has to date, the average person will be flying about in a small mosquito plane, a roadster of the air. The average car will be smaller, safer and more economical. Trains will be shorter, lighter, maintaining more frequent schedules. There will be giant trucks, fleets of trucks, trackless trains. Our grandchildren will travel at

[267]

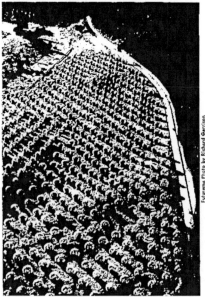

speeds which are unheard of today. Better
farm machinery will reduce production
costs and working hours. New tastes, new
foods will be made possible. New methods
of processing and packing and faster transportation will have improved the quality of
foods. Farms will be feeding factories as
well as mouths. Derivatives of milk are already being used in pharmaceutical, plastic,
paper, dyeing, leather-tanning, carbonated
beverage industries, and we have only begun to find commercial use for skim-milk
and whey-derived by-products.

By 1960 there will probably be many
new industries. Artificial fibers will have
become a major industry. Textile filaments
derived from coal, water and air are stronger
and finer and more elastic than any fiber
now in use. Threads of rubber and glass are
already being woven into cloth. Fabrics
will be poured like paper and made into
clothes so cheap that it won't pay to launder
them. Plastics, clear as glass, strong as steel,
inexpensive as clay, will find new uses in
homes, airplanes, automobiles. Air condi-
tioning and refrigeration of homes will be
as common as heating them. There will be
flameless stoves and rubless washing ma-

SCIENCE IS TEACHING US HOW TO AID NATURE

chines. Telephone, radio, motion pictures and television will have new uses: they may record messages, bulletins and even whole newspapers and books in the home or in the office. In architecture new materials, processes, prefabrication, will tie up with the concept of planning.

One of the most helpful of modern paradoxes is the fact that mechanical industrialism, which during the hundred years of its growth laid waste the land, used up the cities, and bruised the face of everything it touched, now offers as the fruit of its maturity such things as powerful tools, rationalized

Futurama Photo by Richard Garrison

WELL-PLANNED TOWNS WILL FOSTER WELL-PLANNED LIVES

techniques, precision, teamwork. For years there was talk that machinery had enslaved the individual, but now it can free the individual. It can do it most eloquently through housing. The functional sound-proof, air-conditioned room inside the well-planned building is only the beginning. The group of well-planned buildings—the community—is next. The country as a whole will follow. Living in such a world of light, fresh air, open parks, easy movement, the man of 1960 will more naturally play his full part in the community and develop in mind and body.

Some critics predict the doom of the skyscraper. The tall building, far from

BUILDING OF THE FUTURE

Futurama Photo by General Motors

being a Frankenstein, is really a great possibility which we have not yet learned to use. The business center of a town of four thousand inhabitants usually has several blocks of two and three buildings housing its stores, offices and haberdasheries. Doctors and lawyers are spread out. The Mayor's office has its own building. There are the movie theater, the bank, the telegraph office. Each little building has its own management, its heating, its upkeep and its inconveniences for the shoppers who have to go in and out of door after door.

In 1960 the shopper may go into the one tall building in which the whole community will be centered. The doctor will be there, and the butcher, the movie, the mayor, the grocer, the drug store, the pet shop, bank, post office, employment agency. In summer it will be cooled and in winter heated. Instead of six blocks of helter-skelter commercial buildings averaging three stories in height, there will be one block eighteen stories high, thus releasing five whole blocks for parks, playgrounds, parking lots or residential sections. Efficiency and ease will have moved on from city into small town. And paralleling all this, over the whole country, efficient highways will have been laid down. But these highways will not be laid down merely as required. They will have been carefully thought out and planned ahead in preparation for any eventuality.

Many people have a fear of that word "planning." It has been shied away from in alarm as something that implied restriction of the individual. But intelligent planning is the only means by which the individual can fully develop his potentialities and opportunities.

History reveals many examples of successful, intelligent long-range planning. In America, the Founding Fathers laid out a plan of national government that has withstood the changes of time. The history of American industry, often pointed to as a triumph of lack of planning, is also actually a history of brilliant plans which met success. The telephone industry, for example, whose network of wire has broken the isolation of farms, canceled out

[271]

state lines, altered whole ways of doing business and increased the tempo of life, did not descend full-grown upon America; it had to be painstakingly planned, with detailed forethought spent on each aspect of the intricate problem. And in this country today, $110,300,000,000 in life-insurance policies tell in eloquent figures the extent to which individuals plan and make provision for the future.

Today, just as the participation and encouragement of government in the work of science has grown steadily more important, so grows the need of its participation in long-term planning. Thousands of private enterprises, utilities and industries have set up agencies to study and coordinate their work, but none has gone as far as setting down a series of over-all principles. It has remained for government to do this. In 1933 the Federal government, recognizing the need for such thinking in one of its great water-power developments, created the Tennessee Valley Authority, which was to consider all phases of life in the region: problems of the farmers, methods of hydraulics, elementary education, chemical engineering, agriculture, electricity, the rights of seven states within whose lines the project lies, the interests of private companies. The daring of this venture equals its magnitude. It has accomplished under one authority what never could have been done piecemeal, at various times, by various authorities

One of the great corollaries brought out by the TVA was the recognition that in matters concerning natural resources and basic needs state borders can no longer be considered binding. In the past, many states were able to maintain a "splendid isolation," because, for geographic reasons, they felt detached and independent. But when railroads and highways which did not stop at state lines came along, the obvious fact sunk in that neither did rivers, mountains or the problems of land use, conservation and erosion stop at state lines. Planning, which had been almost impossible when people thought purely in terms of political divisions, states, became possible when people began to think in terms of economics. Accordingly, various neighborly groups of states throughout the country have banded together and set up their own Regional Planning Commissions; and the work of these agencies encourages high hope for America's future. The smallest of these, in regard to area administered, is the Port of New York Authority, set up jointly by the States of New York and New Jersey to unify the freight terminals and simplify transportation around their joint harbors. It has built bridges, tunnels and depots, and operates all of them at a steady profit.

In the Far West the Colorado River Basin Compact between seven states, the entire Colorado River area, is vastly greater. In that region, every planning consideration is subsidiary to the securing of an adequate water supply. The development and use of the Colorado River affects the welfare of hundreds of cities, towns and villages containing millions of people. By means of this Interstate Compact and the Federal government's great Boulder Dam project, settlers in the region are protected from floods; they are enabled to irrigate and cultivate hundreds of thousands of otherwise arid acres; they are able to electrify their farms and homes; and they are finding that as a result of those hydro-electric developments, various metallurgical industries are moving into the region. In the Pacific Northwest, a similar Regional Planning Commission has been created for Montana, Idaho, Oregon and Washington. The same set-up exists in New England, where six states have banded together in a planning commission to determine the long-range needs of the whole region.

There are good examples of American planning, then, concerning natural resources and regional surveys, but there has never been an attempt to apply these ideas of planning to systems of transportation. The nearest to planning that a highway engineer ever comes is at a time of crisis when he is suddenly asked to solve a bewildering traffic problem which has arisen only because there

[273]

never was a plan. It is this absence of real highway planning—municipal, state and Federal—that has caused the expenses for streets and roads to be multiplied beyond reason. Planning, with knowledge of the past and thought for the future, is the basis of constitutional government, just as it is an essential part of any industrial management.

The time has come to face the traffic problem as America is learning to face the resources and conservation problems. It can no longer be dealt with by waiting for more developments. Developments have already occurred. Their result is a pressing national emergency. America cannot do less than lay out, with the best forethought it can muster, a system of motorways which twenty years from now will not be a vast lost investment, but an adequate answer to growing needs. If these motorways are to be built, it can be done only under the authority of one great national plan.

A plan to govern the flow and distribution of American motor traffic will concern itself with broad sociological and economic issues. Studies will be made of shifting population, future concentrations, location of vital mineral and agricultural wealth, industrial and agricultural trends in the exploitation of that wealth, in the light of changes that have already begun.

A GREAT DAM FROM AN AMERICAN PLAN—FEDERAL FORESIGHT FOR REGIONS INSTEAD OF STATES   *Fairchild*

Examine a general map of the United States. The population centers of today may not be the same fifty years hence. Cities which now are prosperous may not be so then. Certain centers, like New

York and San Francisco and New Orleans, which lie in superb natural harbors, will not fade in importance; nor will others which contain basic industries or produce terminals. But new cities will arise, as new regions certainly will, and the motorway plan must be so flexibly devised that its coverage can at any time be adapted and extended to take care of new conditions. The opening up of those sections of the United States which are now undeveloped or lightly populated but which, because of their advantages in natural resources, seem destined to future importance, is fundamental to the plan itself. The plan must permit certain sections of the motorway, in case there is no need for them, to be dropped without destroying the basic pattern of high-speed uncongested travel. The plan must consider not only the United States, but the countries to the north and south, and the probable relations of their people to ours. Canada and South America will probably be of more importance to the United States in the future than they are today. Routes will have to be designed to accommodate traffic draining through the United States from Alaska to South America.

Contrary to accepted practice, the motorways must not be laid down using cities as their terminal points, nor must they be allowed to infringe on city boundaries or the city proper. They must connect with cities, ports and industrial centers, as well as with existing inter-urban roads, by means of feeder roads, thus serving population centers without entering the actual concentration points. They must be designed to enlarge the sphere of each individual motor-car operator; to develop road construction into a higher type of industry, using the full knowledge of all phases of engineering, prefabrication, permanent and resilient surfacing, illumination and automatic traffic control. While express motorways must be designed to carry fast, long-distance traffic, no existing roads need be scrapped. The country's 1940 roads will continue to carry local traffic, and their usefulness will be enhanced by connection with

WHERE MOTORWAYS FROM OPPOSITE DIRECTIONS JOIN   Futurama Photo by Richard Garrison

the new motorways, just as rural telephone systems give a wider range of
service when connected to the transcontinental trunk-line network that ex-
tends throughout the country.

On the accompanying map such a Motorway Plan has been worked out.
This plan is based on a relatively brief, preliminary study. But, although it is

necessarily tentative, it is a key to a final comprehensive plan. Its design sums up the basic requirements of such a plan.

This map shows the country's principal population centers. Large black dots represent the larger cities, and cities with smaller population are shown as stars. Every city in the country with a population of 50,000 or over is indicated. The heavy lines represent the routes of the National Motorway System. Fine lines show the tentatively proposed superhighways of the Federal Bureau of Public Roads, for purposes of comparison. The scale on this map is so small that a pin point represents a distance of approximately ten miles. Because of this, only general routes are shown. Motorways won't really converge at the sudden angles which the map suggests. They will overpass and underpass each other, using wide-flowing developments of present-day cloverleafs; their traffic streams in the opposite direction will be completely separated, and individual lanes in the same direction will be segregated by separators. Although on the map they look like solid lines shooting across the country, actually they are complicated mechanisms which differentiate sharply between through traffic and maneuvering traffic, and which provide automatically safe means for entering and leaving the motorways. Their lanes are designed for three separate and constant speeds of 50, 75 and 100 miles an hour. Their grades are constant, never excessive. Their curving radii are constant, and always gen-

Futurama Photo by Richard Garrison

[277]

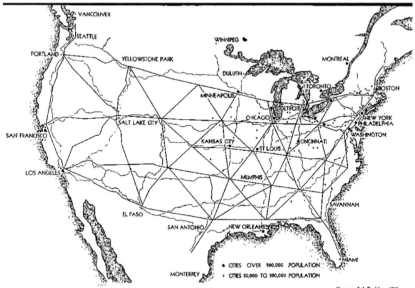

Norman Bel Geddes, 1939

A NATIONAL MOTORWAY PLAN

erous. All over the United States, the motorways are uniform and function in exactly the same way.

The first step which was taken in planning this motorway system was made by laying out lines connecting all cities with populations over 100,000. This resulted in a maze of criss-crossing lines covering the country, dense in heavily congested sections, sparse where cities are spread out. A study of this map showed that there were certain sectional centers of population common to groups of cities. By joining these sectional centers there resulted a series of lines leading from one center to another.

See how directly the lines lead from one region to another. Notice that a direct route connects Seattle and El Paso—making possible uninterrupted

[278]

travel from the northwest tip of the United States to the southernmost section. The various seaports on the Atlantic and Pacific Coasts are directly connected, facilitating overland transportation of imports and exports. The important industrial centers are joined with the seaports. Nowhere do the cities contact the motorways, although they are all fairly close to them. The heaviest route of all avoids Boston, Providence, New York, Philadelphia and Baltimore as it steers straight toward Washington. Traffic moves in almost a straight line from Boston to New Orleans without passing through a single city. Yet no city of over 100,000 is more than 50 miles from a motorway, and most of them are half that distance. The motorways never veer from their course in order to avoid a city. Chicago, Detroit, Los Angeles and New York—all of them are conveniently near these motorways.

Look at the northernmost motorway, which runs east-west across the top tier of states. It starts about 50 miles outside of Boston. It sweeps slightly northward through Central New York toward Rochester, passing Buffalo on the north. It crosses the Niagara River above the falls; without swerving, it hurries through the province of Ontario, crosses Lake St. Clair north of Detroit, avoids Grand Rapids by 35 miles, and makes straight for Lake Michigan. At this point the lake is 50 miles wide. Never mind. There is no let-down on the motorway. It shoots directly across the lake on a long bridge. When it reaches shore, Milwaukee is well off to the south, Sheboygan close by on the north. It heads through the lake and dairy country of Wisconsin, increasing its northerly slant in order to make connections with the Twin Cities. When it moves into the great land of summer wheat, the drivers know they're in the Dakotas. Billings, Montana, dips by to the south, and the Rockies rise ahead. Still the motorway never veers. Its slow lanes may start to wind as it rises into the wild country beyond Butte and Anaconda, but the 100-mile lane darts straight through. All the lanes come off the divide together at the

Columbia River. They head down the steep river basin for Portland. Just before getting there, they meet the great Pacific Coast Motorway and merge in a sweeping non-stop intersection.

In order to realize the ground this route has covered—and the ground that planned engineering has saved it from covering—one had best look at the figures. By airplane, the distance from Boston to Portland is 2,800 miles. On the best 1940 highways, the distance is 3,320 miles—16 per cent longer than by airplane. The motorway distance is about 3,000 miles—only 7 per cent longer than by air! All the routes of the Motorway System—horizontal, vertical and diagonal—are so straightened out over present roads that the air-line route is only 7 per cent straighter.

The result of this National Motorway System is that traffic by car, bus and truck can move swiftly, safely, comfortably and economically over direct rights of way with a sufficient number of lanes to take care of the corresponding volume of traffic. This constitutes a new form of transportation. The principles behind it go beyond the immediate aim of linking sections of the country in the most direct and economical fashion. Another principle is involved:

Futurama Photo by Richard Garrison

to provide ahead of time for each coming half century's traffic growth. That means reaching out into the future of this country, its people, its industries. Therefore it obviously can be organized and built only by full and

GRACEFUL BRIDGES OF HIGH SPEED ROUTES CROSS VALLEYS AND LOWER SPEED LANES

Futurama Photo by Richard Garrison   SIMPLE, EASY GRADES OF THE MOTORWAY IN MOUNTAINOUS TERRAIN

central authority. The organization which goes about this vast work must be a permanent one, as independent of factional politics as the Army and Navy. Implicit in it is the idea of a master plan, and the steps by which that plan is designed must be as carefully determined as the final plan itself. They can be listed as follows:

1) The National Motorway Planning Authority should organize a research and engineering staff to develop its program and to direct and coordinate its work with the individual efforts of state, county and municipal programs.

2) The Authority should collect, analyze and disseminate information about methods of highway construction as observed in all phases of scientific progress.

3) The Authority should develop new ideas and methods to bring about safety, comfort, speed and economy; these findings will be circulated to various construction departments and bureaus for incorporation into the nation's road system.

4) The Authority should provide the nation with a plan that takes into consideration all the best things that have been done in road building so far and superimpose upon them a master Motorway System that will look far into the future.

These steps, suggesting a most careful and studied approach, will be made

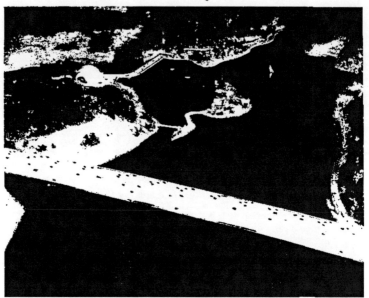

GREAT EXPANSES OF WATER ARE NO HAZARD TO THE MOTORWAY   Futurama Photo by Richard Garrison

even more deliberate by the fact that the National Motorway System will not all be built at once. The "go" signal for the construction of a new motorway will not be given until population flow, traffic density and other considerations indicate its necessity. National survey and research will, however, determine the right of way needed a good while before its construction is actually required, and reserve it for that purpose. This long-range over-all planning will make it possible to secure the rights of way before emergency conditions cause a rise in land values.

This is not an impractical, visionary proposal. Such thorough planning and organization is not unknown today. To cite just one example, refer once more to the telephone industry. Every detail in this industry's intricate organization is anticipated and planned. When a new transcontinental or overseas cable is needed, there is no frantic last-minute rush to collect strands of copper. The cable, the result of years of study and design, is available. The cable has been built long before the need for it became an emergency. A traffic bureau, maintained just to study population movements, informs the company of every change in commercial centers and the focal points of regions. The location of lines is planned in terms of this research.

The same procedure must be followed in road building, because roads are not ends in themselves but means to ends. They depend on and are designed for human enterprise. Other inventions bring the world to us. But the car enables us to go out into the world ourselves. Communication of ideas and emotions thus established has the effect of bringing the country into a closer unity. In this way an enormous influence is brought to bear on the manners and morals of the nation. Old ideas of education are revised; new antidotes for ennui are discovered. Isolated communities are knit together and congested centers can spread out.

Road building must be viewed in an entirely different light than it has been up to now. It has to be considered as something far more than merely providing the means for getting people from one place to the next. The motorways must be considered as an essential part of the entire economic system of the country. The problem of traffic flow is only a step removed from the problems of resources, conservation, national defense, education and unemployment. As the American road builder of the future becomes a planner, he will grow into a key individual who is responsible to the whole nation.

EFFECTS OF A NATIONAL MOTORWAY SYSTEM

15

I T IS standard practice among highway engineers to calculate in figures the results—chiefly in terms of economies in time and fuel consumption—that will come from the building of a new road. With this motorway, the problem is the same only stepped up a thousandfold. The forecasting here rises to a very special plane. For these motorways, when added up together, do not amount to just so many thousand miles of new road. The principles behind their construction are those of freeing traffic and opening up land. What that amounts to isn't just "extension" or "improvement," but actually a new form of transportation.

It has been said before that every new form of transportation is, almost by definition, revolutionary. The effects of revolutions are felt through the entire economy. They may be shocks. They are also likely to be vast advances.

The coming of the automobile itself had revolutionary effects upon American industry. A vast new group of manufacturers came into existence. Millions of men and women found new employment. An undreamed-of increase took place in the production of related industries. Original and ingenious

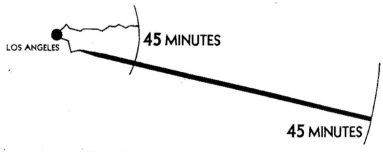

LOS ANGELES **45 MINUTES**

45 MINUTES

A MODERN HIGHWAY SYSTEM WOULD EXTEND A CITY'S COMMUTING RADIUS 6 TIMES

manufacturing methods were devised to fulfill newly created needs. By 1939, it was found that every fifth dollar spent in retail business represented purchases of or for automobiles. An even more impressive indication of the economic value of the automobile was that one out of every seven employed persons in the country was engaged in the motor transport field. Even the competing railroads benefited from the motor industry, carrying one carload of automotive equipment out of every seven carloads of freight.

These were some of the immediate effects of one new industry. The effects of a great motorway system must be calculated on an even broader basis. That the opening of new traffic arteries and the speeding-up of truck and passenger transport will result in greater use of automobiles and of the products that serve them is unquestionable. These new roads are not to be laid down for the motor car alone. As the national motorway system is built, distribution is also built. Travel radius increases. Travel habits are changed. Decentralized communities come into existence, population trends are changed. Cities tend to become centers for working, the country districts centers for living. A demand for new products will be created which may far transcend the mere demand for motor cars. New roads open new communities for new housing. And the motorway system does far more than that. Questions of land use are raised; they may be answered by entire shifts in location of agriculture. With the re-studying of the use of land comes the possibility of tapping new resources. Opportunities are thus made for new industries.

A national motorway system maintaining a high grade of efficiency will maintain the flow of goods to the consumer without interruption. Demand can be more easily predicted; supply will be more uniform, and to that extent business will grow more stable. With expanded markets, prices will become more uniform.

Today only those sections of the country which are served by railroads are of economic consequence. Road development so far has followed population and commercial development, not led it. Roads have left vast tracts of farm land relatively inaccessible. By avoiding difficult mountain terrain, roads have left unopened regions that contain great resources. Every schoolboy knows that America's basic steel industry at the end of the nineteenth century flourished in places where coal was near at hand and to which iron ores could readily be transported. Future schoolboys may have to go further and recite how the new metallurgical industries which became basic toward the middle of the twentieth century grew up in places where hydro-electric power and the ores for alloys were near at hand. The older industry, centered in the Great Lakes basin, had waterways at its disposal, and railroads were built to serve it. The newer industries, moving into the upland of power projects and mountain ores, don't have waterways, and sometimes don't have railways. In 1940 no advantage could be taken of the great source of stored-up water power in the inaccessible mountain lakes scattered all over the country. The great motorways which alone could overcome this isolation hadn't yet been built.

For farmers the twin facts of increased speed and widened radius will be valuable in bringing their produce closer to market, bringing their farms within the orbit of an active economy. In turn, city housewives, buying a staple such as eggs, will not have to depend either on the products of what may be inferior nearby poultrymen or on "fresh" eggs that have taken a week to get to the city, via truck, terminal, train, and then terminal and truck again. High-speed trucks will transport the most perishable foods overnight directly from one point to another, eliminating the in-between delays. That will release many farmers from their age-old attempt to produce a certain fruit or vegetable which another farmer 1,000 miles away can produce far more efficiently. A day may come, indeed, when each piece of land is used only for those crops for which its soil is particularly well suited.

While one is adding up the specific effects which a new motorway system will have, one must not overlook the tourist industry. The American tourist spends billions of dollars a year traveling within his own country. In Florida, tourist trade is vastly more profitable than the basic citrus-fruit industry. In California, it is nearly as important as petroleum. In Michigan, it is second only to automobiles, and in Maine, second only to farming. The principle that drives most tourists is to get as far away from their homes as the usual two-week vacation will permit. A 100-mile-an-hour motorway system will treble their range, opening up new vacation fields.

The essence of the motorway idea is that of new opportunity. A demand for new ways of doing things will create demands for new things themselves. Yesterday's luxuries will be converted into today's necessities. The lifeblood of industry is constant expansion. Economic recovery and prosperity are achieved, not by suppressing industry but by creating more industry. More industry puts more people to work. What holds America back from doing vital deeds today is not, as in some countries, exhaustion or even, primarily,

TERRACED FIELDS TO HOLD THE SOIL

fear of war. There is no lack of individual courage. But there exists a certain public suspicion of united effort. No one denies that America is strong and rich, that it has vast possibilities, but people dispute about the ways in which America might realize these possibilities. The land is vast, and so are its problems. But vaster still are the rewards which will come to the generation that ceases to shrink from great vision and great labor. People will see that if roads are designed specifically for their traffic, then whole cities too ought to be designed specifically for the business of cities. It is not the business of cities to serve as residential centers. It is their business to serve as occupational units, nerve-centers, headquarters. Then they should be designed as such.

The obverse of this is that the same kind of thinking will be applied to the residential areas as they move out from congestion, bad air and blight. People will learn that the method of dividing suburbs into square blocks fronted with tight rows of houses doesn't make them suburbs at all, but just transplanted cities. When new outlying communities are built, they will be planned long before the houses go up. Streets out of reach of through traffic, underpasses for pedestrians, and dwellings will be set to take advantage of topography, the position of the sun, the prevailing currents of the air. Outdoor recreation will not be provided for as an afterthought. Apply this thinking to a mill town along the Monongahela River, where thousands of families live alongside the grimy mills. Those towns were set up when transportation was difficult. With an adequate highway system to transport them back and forth, these families could be moved 30 to 50 miles away from their place of work. A day will come when factory labor lives not in shanties on the other side of the tracks, but in healthy uplands between forest and stream.

Farms will center around what might be called an agricultural terminal, managed by the community of farmers for the common purposes of storing, selling, and shipping. Rural isolation will give way to rural cooperation.

By eliminating friction and the jams in social life today, planning makes for health—not alone the physical health that one may expect from decentralization and free movement, but for mental health as well. The sociologist Charles H. Cooley merely reiterated a widely felt suspicion when he stated, "The extreme concentration of population at centers has deplorable effects upon the health, intelligence and morals of people." When the time comes and transportation finally realizes its purpose—namely, to free men from bondage to their immediate surroundings—it is not only their bodies that will be restored by sun and air and contact with nature. It is their minds as well.

Motoring is one of the most popular recreations there is. It promotes the sense of freedom that comes from greater mobility. It introduces variety,

LOCAL ROADS FEED INTO THE MOTORWAY

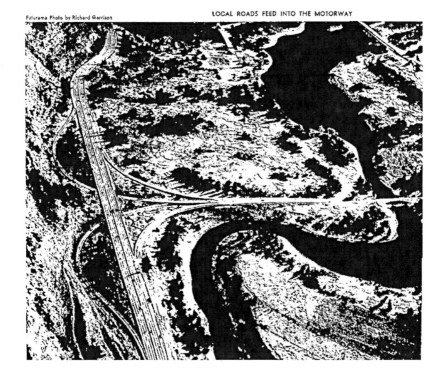

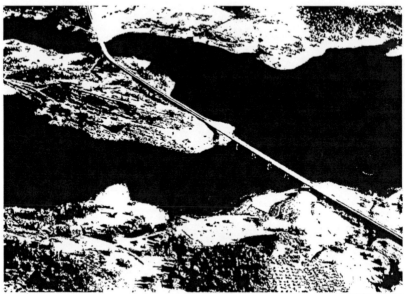

THE NATIONAL MOTORWAY CROSSES A LARGE LAKE   Futurama Photo by Richard Garrison

change of scenery, a greater social diffusion, a widening of the horizon.

This freedom of movement, this opening up of what is congested, this dis-
carding of what is obsolete all add up to one thing: *interchange*—interchange of people, places, ways of life, and therefore modes of thought. The
American nation is not going to be able to solve the major problems facing it
until its people of various classes and regions—the workers, the intellectuals,
the farmers, the business men—get to know each other better and to under-
stand each other's problems.

An America in which people are free, not in a rhetorical sense, but in the
very realistic sense of being freed from congestion, waste and blight—free to
move out on good roads to decent abodes of life—free to travel over routes
whose very sight and feel give a lift to the heart—that is an America whose

[294]

MODEL FARMS WILL SEEK LOCATIONS ADJACENT TO THE MOTORWAYS FOR QUICKER DISTRIBUTION

inner changes may far transcend the alterations on the surface. If city dweller can know the land, Easterner know Westerner, the man who has lived among mountains know harbors and the sea, then horizons will be broadened, individual lives will grow. Along with the interchange, there will be plenty of diversity. And diversity—whether racial or geographic—is a basic heritage of America. And out of that very interchange of diversity will come another thing—something which in this era of misunderstanding and conflict and war may be the most essential thing of all. Our country was founded on it. We call it *unity*. It is not a unity imposed from above, such as exists under dictatorship, but a unity based on freedom and understanding.

A national motorway system will have still another important effect. It will supplement American military defense. Mobility has always been the keynote of warfare from the beginning of time, and today with the highly mechanized transport developments in military machines this factor reaches its highest importance. The value of military machines increases in direct ratio to the value of the roadway over which they maneuver. An army which can arrive at a point of attack in the shortest possible time is an efficient army. Delay is fatal. Artillery equipment which cannot be moved to a danger zone quickly when it is needed is useless artillery. The national motorway system would enable almost instantaneous transport of men and equipment to any point in the nation, east, west, north or south. The bulk of our military force could be shifted from one extreme section of the country to another in a day or two at the most. Fast and efficient air service could not accomplish this because it is too expensive and because it cannot handle the great bulk required. Fast and efficient train service would not be adequate either, because the train is not as flexible a vehicle as the motor car. Furthermore, an express motorway system of this nature would avoid all cities and towns, which would not only have the effect of speeding up the mobilization but of spreading it out, helping to avoid the dangerous concentration of men and equipment which makes war against innocent civilians in cities such a ghastly aspect of modern war. Really fast land transportation without danger of accidents could well be the number one asset of a military defense system.

Many aspects of military defense must be regarded as an unfortunate necessity because they serve no positive, creative peaceful function—they do not

SUCH SUSPENSION BRIDGES MAY BE POSSIBLE WITH THE INCREASING KNOWLEDGE OF ENGINEERING

Futurama Photo by Richard Garrison

provide us with more food, better housing, better health, better working conditions, more economic security. In fact, money has to be spent on them which might otherwise be spent on internal improvements. But national motorways are at one and the same time both an effective instrument of military defense and a constructive aid in internal improvement.

We all hope that America will not become involved in Europe's tragic war. Let us build American motorways which will help us to stay out and which will, at the same time, help us make the most of this country's peace-time resources.

> To carry buildings and streets with you afterward wherever you go,
> To gather the minds of men out of their brains as you encounter them, to gather the love out of their hearts,
> To take your lovers on the road with you, for all that you leave them behind you,
> To know the universe itself as a road, as many roads, as roads for traveling souls.
>
> —WALT WHITMAN